SCREENWRITING
Behind Enemy Lines

LESSONS FROM INSIDE THE STUDIO GATES

by
John Schimmel

MICHAEL WIESE PRODUCTIONS

Published by Michael Wiese Productions
12400 Ventura Blvd. #1111
Studio City, CA 91604
(818) 379-8799, (818) 986-3408 (FAX)
mw@mwp.com
www.mwp.com

Cover design: Johnny Ink www.johnnyink.com
Cover photo: Mati Young
Copy editor: Matt Barber
Interior layout: Jay Anning
Printed by McNaughton & Gunn

Manufactured in the United States of America

Library of Congress Cataloging-in-Publication Data

Schimmel, John, 1948-
Screenwriting behind enemy lines : lessons from inside the studio gates / John Schimmel.
     pages cm
  ISBN 978-1-61593-167-5 (pbk.)
  1. Motion picture authorship--Handbooks, manuals, etc. I. Title.
PN1996.S3375 2014
808.2'3--dc23
                                        2013033124

"Attention to those crazy enough to consider being a screenwriter: Save yourself some pain. *Screenwriting Behind Enemy Lines* is a savvy, smart insiders guide to screenwriting. John Schimmel has honestly delivered important insights showing us what it takes to connect audiences to classic stories and characters while road mapping how it is achieved with first-hand intimacy."
— ANDREW DAVIS, director, *The Fugitive, Collateral Damage, A Perfect Murder,* and *Holes*

"I have often said that John is the best story executive in the business. He has an uncanny knack in developing and fixing narrative and character and in a collaborative field is often the only person in the development room who can somehow fathom the solution to an intractable problem with either. John is an extraordinarily gifted story analyst and himself a vivid writer with a truly cinematic eye."
— PETER SAMUELSON, producer (*Arlington Road*); director of Media Institute for Social Change, USC Film School

"Highly recommended. Schimmel's exploration of character and story development is invaluable. The exercises at the end of each chapter help writers to apply what they've read to their screenplays, which can help add depth to scripts that might otherwise be viewed as formulaic."
— WENDY MOORE, Full Sail University faculty and StayForTheCredits.net host

"With real experience in the business, author John Schimmel has crafted one of the most essential references in understanding how a good screenplay becomes not only a great screenplay, but also a marketable one."
— STEFAN BLITZ, *Forces of Geek*

"Exploring film from the inside... the inside of the studio, the inside of the writer's mind, and the inside of produced screenplays. John Schimmel's book will help turn your screenplay inside out, and make it better than it was before."

> — MATTHEW TERRY, filmmaker/screenwriter/teacher, reviewer for MicroFilmmaker.com

"In my experience, there are very few people in Hollywood who really understand screenwriting on a profound level. John is one of the few. Being a good screenwriter is not necessarily the same thing as being a successful one. If you read this book you will understand the difference."

> — LIONEL WIGRAM, producer and "story by" credit on the Robert Downey, Jr. *Sherlock Holmes* films and executive producer on five of the *Harry Potter* films

"John Schimmel reveals the truth about how Hollywood makes its cinematic sausage — if you're going to throw your creative soul into the meat grinder, you'll need to read this book."

> — MARK HASKELL SMITH, screenwriter, *Star Trek: Voyager*, *Martial Law*

"The navigation guide on how to tell your story and get it made for the big screen."

> — DAVE WATSON, editor, Movies Matter, davesaysmoviesmatter.com

"Learn how to analyze your story, characters, and dialogue the way Hollywood insiders will. Armed with Schimmel's advice, you'll swim right across the Rubicon and never look back."

> — MARY J. SCHIRMER, screenwriter-editor-instructor, Screenplayers.net

TABLE OF CONTENTS

ACKNOWLEDGMENTS   ix

HOW TO USE THIS BOOK   x

A BRIEF INTRODUCTION   xiii

CHAPTER 1
STUFF YOU SHOULD KNOW BEFORE YOU START   1

The current state of development   2

Your screenplay's journey from submission to green light   5

The only question that matters   6

Criteria for answering the only question that matters   7

What draws people into the theater?   10

Analyzing the success of *Transformers*   19

The Avengers versus *Green Lantern*   21

What *The Avengers*, *Transformers*, and
Little Miss Sunshine have in common   23

Take it to the wall: *Monster's Ball*   24

What it all means to you   27

EXERCISES
Getting started   27

CHAPTER 2
WHAT DRIVES A FILM:
    A prepatory look under the hood   29

What is a scene?   32

The rhythm of reverses   33

Character creation — a quick primer   35

The process for moving forward   36

EXERCISES
Nailing down the basics   37

CHAPTER 3

ACT ONE — STRUCTURE:

   Lessons from the near-death of *The Fugitive*   39

Act One story points   40

Analysis — Act One of *The Fugitive*   43

A tale from the trenches: What the studio didn't understand
about *The Fugitive* and how it nearly killed the film   46

   EXERCISES
   Act One structure/begin your outline   48

CHAPTER 4

A DEEPER DIVE INTO ACT ONE:

   Creating great characters   50

Setting up your protagonist/Creating castable roles   50

Character contradiction   51

Do audiences need to love protagonists?   57

Tools of characterization   59

The relationship between structure and character   68

Other important character issues for Act One   69

Entrances   71

Secondary characters   72

   EXERCISES
   Creating your character bible   74

CHAPTER 5

ACT TWO:

   How *Outbreak* became a film   76

Other components of Act Two   78

The rhythm of Act Two   80

Tips from the pits of development hell —
creating an Act Two that doesn't unravel   81

Analysis — Act Two of *The Fugitive*   82

Another tale from the trenches: *Outbreak* —
How a key Act Two decision won a war between studios   88

An additional lesson from *Outbreak*   94

EXERCISES
Construct your Act Two/Continue your outline   94

CHAPTER 6
ACT THREE:
   Face/Off— A terrifying preview
   and what it has to teach   97

Analysis — Act Three of *The Fugitive*   98

A third tale from the trenches — The first preview of *Face/Off*   100

A brief digression about trailer moments   102

A note about writing your first draft   103

EXERCISES
Design an Act Three that's worth the wait   103

CHAPTER 7
REWRITING AND REVISING:
   First drafts are never as great as you think   107

The eight rules of the rewrite process   109

The clearest clues that you have a ways to go   115

Be your own script whisperer:
Discovering your screenplay's hidden truth   117

Making peace with ceding control
to your own subconscious   119

How to sabotage your own rewrite —
Self-destructive writers I have known   122

EXERCISES
Getting ready for your rewrite   123

CHAPTER 8

THE POLISH:
   Wordsmithing your screenplay   128

When are you ready to polish?   128

Word choice — the poetry of screenwriting   128

Shaping your paragraphs   131

The dialogue polish   133

Description and Action   136

Scenes   145

Length   146

Title   148

Proofreading — The final step of the polish   148

EXERCISES
Polishing your screenplay   149

CHAPTER 9

A CLOSER LOOK:
   Little Miss Sunshine, The King's Speech, Lincoln   151

The ensemble film: *Little Miss Sunshine*   151

The King's Speech: No, the flawed hero is not his own antagonist   167

Rules are made to be broken: The screenplay for *Lincoln*   189

EXERCISES
Do what I just did   201

CHAPTER 10

FINAL THOUGHTS:
   Lessons from Bob Dylan and the Internet   202

EXERCISES
Examine what you've learned   211

ABOUT THE AUTHOR   212

ACKNOWLEDGMENTS

My thanks go to Jule Selbo who has been a mentor and friend for more years than I care to admit and who steered me toward my first teaching job at UCLA Extension. To Tod Goldberg who runs the extraordinary UC Riverside Low Residency MFA Program in Creative Writing and Writing for the Performing Arts and whose encouragement based on an early draft of this book was invaluable. To Ken Lee of Michael Wiese Productions for his patience guiding me to the final version of the book. And especially to my wife Maureen and my kids Gabe, Grace, and Amelia, who are my inspiration and my heroes.

HOW TO USE THIS BOOK

This book is intended to help you through the process of writing a screenplay, from idea to polished draft. It starts with an overview of the business and tries to give an insider's sense of the not-necessarily intuitive things that financiers and filmmakers look for when they read your script. It may come as a surprise that "art" — what you have to say — is emphasized at least as much as craft.

Chapter One makes a strong case for why now more than ever you need to submit only the most "finished" version of your screenplay. The exercises that follow Chapter One push you to start looking at films — and at your own ideas — as a working screenwriter.

Chapter Two allows you to get your feet wet in the basics of screenplay structure and character development, with exercises to help you start to translate your idea and characters into the pieces you'll need to create a first draft.

Chapters Three through Six go into screenplay construction in detail. Both Chapters Three and Four focus on the first thirty pages — Act One — because I believe that so much of the health of any script depends on what gets set up in this section. Chapters Five and Six are about Act Two and Act Three. Taken together, the exercises that follow these chapters are designed to help you create an outline and character bible to guide the writing process.

If you are just starting a screenplay, I might skip from the end of Chapter Six to Chapter Ten to read the analyses of *Lincoln*, *The King's Speech*, and *Little Miss Sunshine*. In the body of the book I focus on *The Fugitive* as my prime example, partly because I know it intimately, but mostly because it is the clearest example I know of to illustrate the basics of screenwriting. Each film dissected in Chapter Ten was chosen to illustrate a different aspect of screenwriting and hopefully will give you an even more nuanced view of the craft before you start to write.

Once you finish your draft, I would dive back into Chapters Seven through Ten. (Yes, I'd read those breakdowns again.) These chapters are meant to guide your rewrites and polishes — I use the plural there because there will undoubtedly be more than one rewrite and more than one polish.

Chapter Seven is there to help you get into the right frame of mind for the rewrite and for dealing with notes. Chapter Eight ends with a guide through your rewrite, with exercises to help you generate your own development notes. Chapter Eight does the same thing for the polish step.

In Chapter Nine I walk you through a close analysis of three films: *Little Miss Sunshine* to look at ensemble film, *The King's Speech* to look for the antagonist in a film that pits the protagonist against himself, and *Lincoln* to look at a script that breaks a lot of rules. Chapter Ten contains some final thoughts that I hope you find inspiring to go the distance so you can create the best possible version of your script. The exercises that follow these scripts are intended to help you recap all that you have learned.

If you have one or two screenplays that have been sold but not produced, or if you are stuck in an ongoing draft, then I would come at this book somewhat differently. Chances are you are either stuck in the notes process or the financier has lost his/her way. In this case I might start at Chapter Seven and run those exercises as a diagnostic tool. The likelihood is that any issues you are having stem from Act One, so I would pay particular attention to the exercises concerning those pages. The first section goes in depth into the question asked by all producers and studio executives about all scripts — "Is it a movie?" — and so is a good place to start to try and discover what it is you or they might be missing. I would also study Chapters 2.1 and 2.2, the in-depth analysis of a screenplay's first thirty pages, because so many of the issues that can halt a script's progress originate in Act One. And then I'd use Section Three as a guide for rediscovering the instinct that led you to write the project in the first place and for getting back into the rewrite.

Even though this book is written from the point of view of a studio insider, it also comes from the perspective of someone who loves the writing process for what it can give both the writer and the reader. Your goal should be to sell something, but also to say something. I just read that writer George Saunders views a piece of good writing as a black box the reader enters in one emotional state but leaves transformed. I think that's true as well for great films of any genre. In my mind, writing is a spiritual journey. But that can be hard to hold onto when faced with the demands of the business. This book is intended to help you write screenplays that can be sold and produced, but it is at the same time a guide to discovering and making the best use of the Truth that resides in your script.

A BRIEF INTRODUCTION

I feel your pain.

The first screenplay I ever wrote was a piece about nuclear terrorism that was optioned by Fox. I was put up for three months in a swanky hotel while my writing partner and I addressed the studio notes. I knew nothing about writing, but I felt wise enough about the madness of Hollywood to avoid thinking the sale meant anything beyond that sale. We just did the work and avoided thinking we'd taken the first step toward "making it" in Hollywood. We barely paid any attention when it was announced that the studio had been purchased by conservative oilman Marvin Davis.

We turned our rewrite in on a Friday. On Monday morning our producer phoned to say both he and our executive loved it. They were about to sit down and hammer out a directors list.

This was when I finally decided to admit that the script might become a film. I allowed myself a moment of joy. That, apparently, was the signal the gods of mischief had been waiting for.

That afternoon, a friend and I went to celebrate at Harry's Bar in Century City. At 4:30 I called our producer to get the latest news. He was sorry he hadn't phoned. He had some bad news. The studio had abandoned the project and put it into turnaround.

So I have firsthand experience with the fact that the film business is often incomprehensible. But I eventually wound up on the "other side of the desk" with a long and fairly successful career as a studio executive and producer. I have had the privilege to work with wonderful writers, from newbies to Oscar winners and to do a fair amount of un-credited writing myself. And what I have discovered is that, although people like to define Hollywood as a place where stories like mine are common, in fact over the course of my twenty-five years in the business that experience was unique. Not that weird, inexplicable disappointments aren't inevitable. Show business is a gambler's game. But like in any game, there are ways to better the odds. The truth is, as a writer there are clear paths to having some control of your fate if you are informed and really willing to dig in and do the work. At the end of the day, the best defense is the same as the best offense — a great screenplay. And it is well within your power to deliver that.

My goal in this book is to use all I have learned over my years in the business to give you the tools you can use to realize your dream of becoming a working, sought-after screenwriter. And I want for you to come away with a deep understanding of story and of writing that will make you valuable not only as a screenwriter but as a creative force as we move ever deeper into the world of trans-media. This book asks you to focus on three basic things (not necessarily in this order): the Truth that energizes your writing, the craft that allows you to get that Truth on the page in a compelling story with memorable characters, and the nature and demands of the business for which you are writing. So here we go.

> He who works with his hands is a laborer.
> He who works with his hands and his head is a craftsman.
> He who works with his hands and his head and his heart is an artist.
>
> — Saint Francis of Assisi

STUFF YOU SHOULD KNOW BEFORE YOU START

I tried for a while to participate in screenwriters' chat rooms. I wanted to know what was on the minds of budding dramatists. What I found was too many participants lamenting the impossibility of breaking into Hollywood. "You have to know someone," they said. If you weren't connected, you were doomed. To these writers, this was the only acceptable explanation for the "mediocre material" that was being optioned and produced instead of their own screenplays. It was otherwise utterly impossible to understand what "they" were looking for.

Well, I am one of the "theys" and I am here to tell you that that is simply not the case. There is just not a lot of great material that does not either get optioned or recognized as the writing sample of an exciting new voice. The readers who get first crack at your material rejoice when it is good regardless of who the writer might be related to because, to speak frankly, it gives them a break from the sea of soul-crushingly mediocre scripts. This is not entirely the fault of the writers. Screenwriting, like all writing, is tough, and there are too many gurus pedaling pure craft in lieu of giving equal emphasis to content and artistry. But I pretty much guarantee that if you write a great script, it will be recognized.

The deck is not stacked against you. What is unarguable, though, is that the bar has been raised regarding what will be judged as interesting.

Let's start with two facts of life in Hollywood today:

• Great ideas are a dime a dozen. There are just too many unlikely premises that have turned into important films to think otherwise.

• The era of the development deal is basically dead. This, by the way, does not mean that a buyer won't develop your script once they option it. It does mean that the time when financiers spent money on under-cooked screenplays simply because they saw the germ of a good idea is over.

To cut to the chase: If you want a career as a screenwriter in today's market, you have to acquire the means to turn your great idea into a great screenplay. And you have to understand what "great" means within the context of your first audience — the readers who have the power to put your script into the pipeline that can lead to production.

The current state of development

We had a dozen script readers back when I ran the Story Department at Warner Bros. These were union readers, which meant that their workload was proscribed by the union. They could cover two screenplay submissions per day, or one book, or one project in development. So for the sake of argument, let's say that averages out to a submissions load of a script and a half per day per reader. That totals out to ninety submissions per week that were covered. If we multiply that out over the year, taking out a week each for Christmas and Thanksgiving, that's 4,500 submissions per year that came in to Warner Bros.

In 2011, Warner Bros. released something like sixteen films. Taken as a percentage of submissions, that's 0.4%. Even if I am off and only half that many screenplays were submitted, that's still less than 1%. Not great odds.

Back in those days you could still make a pretty good living as a screenwriter even if you had never seen a word you'd written hit the screen. In the early '90s, Warner Bros. had a huge development slate of its own plus a proliferation of director, actor, and producer overhead deals that each came with a development fund. Money was flowing, and screenplays were regularly optioned based on the idea alone, even if the script was nowhere close to working. But that couldn't last.

When I was story editor there was a lovely gentleman called Ralph Peterson who was the studio controller. Ralph was very careful with every dime the studio spent, which is why I was called to his office every couple of months so he could ask me to stop over-tipping at business lunches.

I only had one series of meetings with Ralph that were at my request. The script archives — all of the screenplays and manuscripts that Warner Bros. had ever optioned or purchased, and all of the drafts of all of the projects that had ever been developed — were stored on open shelves in a giant fenced-in locker in the basement of the studio's prop shop. There was considerable concern that the archives were deteriorating, and I had asked to meet with Ralph to petition for a climate-controlled storage facility. Ralph politely heard me out and then presented me with his own solution.

"Burn them," he said.

"Excuse me?" I asked.

"Burn them," he repeated. "If you don't, someone will dig through them, find a project they want to re-activate, and lose us a fortune. Just burn them."

You have to remember that this was the studio that at one time decided it was great idea to dump all of the animation cells from the golden years of Looney Tunes into an incinerator and torch them rather than spend money on storage. So, I was horrified to realize, Ralph meant business.

Warner Bros. eventually did build a new facility for the archives. The thing is, though, from a purely pragmatic, bottom-line point of view I have to admit that there was logic on Ralph's side. In terms of pure percentages, the development group's track record was just not that great — though to be fair, when the process worked it worked spectacularly well. But it was often the case that we'd buy a script because we saw something in it that the writer didn't see or couldn't render. We'd discover that the raw material simply wouldn't support the new vision of the script no matter how many new writers we threw at the project. It was no one's fault, really, but too often it was like buying a Volkswagen and trying to retrofit it into a fighter jet, often with mechanics (a.k.a. new writers) who instead saw it as a tank. With all the great intentions in the world, more often than not what we got was a messed up Volks. Not only was it not a fighter jet, but it was no longer drivable as a car. The archives were filled with those Frankensteins.

Steve Ross ran the parent company in those days. Ross understood and had sympathy for the creative process, and he gave his executives plenty of leeway. But Ross passed away in 1992 and the post-merger studio fell under the control of the corporate boys and girls from Time Warner.

Almost as soon as Ross was buried, longtime studio chiefs Bob Daly and Terry Semel had their suite of offices re-designed so they felt more "corporate." More importantly, they moved the film division's creative group from the main building with its fabulously serpentine corridors and varied offices and stuck us on the second floor of the retrofitted wardrobe building. We were in carefully measured offices on two perpendicular corridors, one of which was directly over the new Warner store. The symbolism could not have been more clear.

In this new corporate environment the fiscal folks looked at the film group's books for development and basically said, "Are you out of your minds?" The change was not instantaneous, of course, but it was relentless. The studios figured out that most of those overhead deals and all of that development was just not all that productive. Today, most of those producer and actor overhead deals that supported so many development deals are gone, as is the studio's appetite to "roll the dice" on under-cooked scripts requiring lengthy development periods. Indeed, one studio has even instituted a policy that offers financial incentives to its development group for taking a script from option to green light in less than one year.

Your screenplay's journey
from submission to green light

I want to digress for a moment and describe the process your screenplay will undergo if you are lucky enough to get an agent or manager to start submitting it around for you. There are various versions of this process, but something like this happens for every script above a certain budget range.

So your agent sends your screenplay either directly to financiers or to producers to see who gets to take it into the various financiers — studios, indies, etc. It eventually gets sent to the executives with whom the producer or agent has a relationship, but unless you are one of the hot writers of the moment the script is immediately sent to the story department. There it is logged in and given to a reader. If the reader likes it, then a junior executive will read it, and so on up the food chain.

Scripts of interest are usually discussed at an afternoon meeting where they are divided up for the weekend read. At some point — if you are lucky — someone will decide it's a movie, the piece will be optioned, tweaked, and then considered for green light.

At a certain point your script will also be evaluated both by the studio's marketing department and the strategic planning group as well as the production group. Strategic planning will run an ROI model — that's Return On Investment. How much might it make at various budget ranges with various levels of cast? And even if they love it, more times than not the answer will come back that the green light is yours so long as the film attracts one of four actors and one of six directors.

That is a lot of people who have to read your script and understand its potential. And, basically, you have exactly one shot with each of them. So it is crucial that the read be as compelling as you can possibly make it. All of the rules of screenwriting I am about to invoke, all of the restrictions that may at first seem frustrating, all of the things I am going to tell you that you need to keep in mind — these lessons are all designed to help you make your readers care deeply enough to keep your story moving toward the screen.

The only question that matters

Ultimately, at every step along the way as your screenplay works its way up the various food chains, there is only one question that matters: **Is it a movie?** What this means in practical terms is that your screenplay has more than one task to accomplish.

Everyone knows that a script is a blueprint for a film. Of course this is true; it's what dictates its peculiar form. This form, by the way, comes from the pragmatic needs of production. At the beginning of any production there is a giant meeting with all the department heads, the director, and the producers. By then the script will have been broken down by days and nights, by interiors and exteriors, by locations, by cast, prop, set, sound and action demands. Actors, with any luck, will have read the script and started learning their lines and, more, they will have begun to form their characters based on how they behave and who they interact with. All of this is laid out in screenplay format in ways that allow all of these people to quickly find what they need.

But before a script becomes a film, it is a sales tool. Remember, your screenplay's first audience will not be the people who will go to see it in the theaters or rent it or tune it in or stream it on their delivery device of choice. The first audience will be made up of the people who will determine if your film ever makes it to one of those platforms in the first place.

Who makes up this first audience? Most of the time it's the gate-keepers for the money and talent — producers, studio executives, marketing folks, agents, managers, and the readers who help them all deal with the flood of material cascading around them. They will all ask the same question: "Is this a movie?" Which is a catch-all for a bucket-full of questions: Who is the audience for this film? Is there a marketing hook? Will it attract talent? Will its cost justify itself? Does it have something interesting to say? Which all boils down to: "Will recommending it get me fired?"

The folks we're talking about are usually guarding highly sought-after people, people you want to consider putting a significant amount of their time and passion into realizing your vision instead of the vision of the zillions of other writers whose scripts are piled up on their desks, bed stands, floors, and kitchen counters. You have to make them think it will be worth their while, because without them you can't get your film financed. So your job is to create a document that convinces them you've got the goods.

Although I suspect that this all sounds crass to the uninitiated, in fact these two agendas — to write a great film and to write a great sales tool — are perfectly linked. Your script will be better for thinking of it both from the point of view of the studio and the talent, assuming that you hang onto your sense of what kind of film you are writing. It is more castable if your characters stand for something. And it will be better for knowing who the audience is. This is decidedly not the same as pandering to an audience. Pandering would be writing something simply because you think it will please your audience. What I'm talking about is writing to your point in a way that speaks to the audience you're chasing — and not writing in a way that will offend it. Knowing who you're writing for will help you hone in on a tone and voice. And, frankly, it will help prevent you from wasting your time.

Criteria for answering the only question that matters

The rocket fuel of a studio executive's life is made up of two parts: the ability to accurately answer the question "Is it a movie?" and then the ability to package the project if the answer is "Yes." Packaging is outside the scope of this book — though to be honest one of the changes in the business is that more and more the studios want writers to arrive with packaged projects. But the question "Is it a movie?" is important and multi-layered. And it is a question with which writers should be familiar.

The answer often depends upon context. There was a single week early in my career as a reader at Warner Bros. when I gave a mediocre screenplay a rare "definitely recommend" but passed on what remains one of the best scripts I have ever read: *Howards End*, adapted from the E.M. Forster novel by the brilliant screenwriter Ruth Prawer Jhabvala.

Howards End was a nearly perfect script that went on to win the Oscar for Best Adapted Screenplay — and I passed on it. Why? Because it was a perfect script for a small, artsy movie that would have gotten lost in the Warner Bros. marketing and distribution machine. The studio would not have had to spend a lot on the production, but that was not the point. The point was that the "machine" would not have known how to sell the film, and so the investments in production and prints and advertising and marketing and distribution would have added up to a substantial loss. The mediocre script, on the other hand, was a spectacular idea for an actor with whom Warner Bros. had an overall deal — and in those days the studio was willing to develop from a screenplay that needed that much work. And in that case the process worked and the movie was a hit.

My point is not that great writing is irrelevant. (Remember, *Howards End* did get made into a wonderful film that found its audience.) Rather, my point is that unless you are planning to self-finance your project, you are writing for a marketplace and you'd better know your customers.

In keeping this in mind, balance is essential. Too much consciousness of the commercial prospects of your project can be just as deadly as too little. For me, the trick is to separate out the reason you choose a project to write from the things you need to keep in mind once the writing has begun. You need to love the projects you work on for their own merit. If you choose something simply because it feels like a combination of the last three hit films you've seen, it will invariably fail. On the other hand, if you can find a project that you love and do what you can to make it marketable, so much the better. Because the fact is, there can be Truth in any idea and Truth is what attracts the artists with whom you want to collaborate to get your film made.

A case in point: Lionel Wigram was one of the smarter executives at Warner Bros. He has great taste, he is himself a skilled writer and filmmaker — and he's the guy who talked the studio into picking up the Harry Potter franchise. (That's right, talked them into it.

Everyone else in town passed.) He loves big stories that take audiences on big adventures. He loves smart. He loves witty. "Loves" as in he is genuinely passionate about films that deliver these things.

When Lionel transitioned out of the executive suite and into a producing deal at Warner Bros. he knew he wouldn't have the funds to compete for the big spec scripts or books. At the same time, he knew he needed to come out of the gate with a project that would fit into the Warner Bros. machine. So he combed through the lists of material that had come into the public domain — chose Sherlock Holmes — and then delivered a comic book with his "modern" take on the material. The choice of material was hard-nosed business, but the way he spun the story had all the elements he loved — scope, wit, adventure, and the scale of a Warner Bros. film. The rest is history.

So, here are the specific elements that make me think a screenplay is a movie:

- I look for a script that creates characters who carry burdens we share or live out fantasies we'd like to share; that takes those characters on compelling, near-impossible journeys to release that burden or live that fantasy.

- I look for a script that tells a story with something at stake that I think will be important to its audience.

- I look for writers who value what they have to say and say it in a way that is coherent and respectful of its audience.

- I look for a script in which the writer shows real mastery over his/her subject. Does the screenplay read like stars and directors will have confidence in the writer?

- I look for scripts in which the roles seem castable. How are the leads introduced? How much of the action do they drive? How compelling are the obstacles he or she has to overcome to get to their goal? Is there a powerful theme that is expressed through the actions of the characters? Does the climax justify the journey?

- I look for screenplays that point at a clear target audience. I worked with a writer who wrote a beautiful film that included dragons, a depressed adult author, and a terminally ill young boy. I loved that script, but getting it financed proved impossible because no one could figure out who the audience would be.

There is something else, a certain sense of mastery and confidence that comes with REALLY knowing what you're doing. It is the same with actors' auditions. Experienced people can often tell if they'll want to work with an actor from the way he or she takes the stage or enters the room. We have to watch the entire audition to get a sense if he or she is right for the role. But we can tell almost immediately if there is even a possibility.

In a similar vein, there is something that develops when one has read a zillion scripts, a sort of sixth sense. Some readers say they can tell within the first ten pages if a writer has what it takes to deliver something of interest. I once read the opening paragraph of a script and wrote in the margin, "This owns me already." That screenplay, by the way, went on to win second place in the UCLA Extension screenwriting competition. There is a kind of alchemy that occurs when a writer's mastery permeates the script. The converse is also true — a lack of mastery is nearly impossible to mask.

What draws people into the theater?

This, of course, is the billion-dollar question. What draws an audience to a piece of work? Screenwriter William Goldman (*Butch Cassidy and the Sundance Kid*, *The Princess Bride*, *Marathon Man*) famously answered this question in his book *Adventures in the Screen Trade* with the line, "No one knows anything." And to some extent he's right — even wildly successful studios, producers, and directors have the occasional spectacular misstep.

Still, the important question for you to ask yourself is this: Especially in this era when stars don't guarantee success and even the best trailer moments — the moments when something spectacular or captivating or intriguing happens that you can cut into the trailer — can't on their own deliver or satisfy an audience, is there stuff you as a writer can provide that will attract an audience? My answer is a rousing, "Yes!"

Back when I was leading another life, I was part of a group of musicians who improvised a score for director Arthur Penn's film *Four Friends*. Penn had directed *Bonnie and Clyde* and *Little Big Man* and we were relatively clueless neophytes in the film scoring kingdom. Penn would have been entitled to behave like a diva. But he was interested in experimenting and in the artistic sensibility of Elizabeth Swados, the woman I was working with, and he could not have been a more generous or genial collaborator.

Penn, now in his eighties, has, along with everyone else I know with any history in the film business, become sort of cranky about it. Penn wrote a column for the December 5, 2012, issue of *The NYC Actor* called "No Friction. No Interest. No Play." He was writing about the theater, but makes clear that his comments apply in a larger context:

> There is very little art, but there is a great deal of boosterism. Fill the seats; buy a T-shirt; post something on the Internet; send out an e-mail blast... I don't want to just shit on the theatre: It's bad everywhere, because it's all business, real-estate space with actors. It's no longer something vital. I used to think that the theatre was like a good newspaper: It provided a service; people wanted and needed it; revenue was provided by advertisers who bought space if the paper delivered, but profit was not the motive — the motive was the dissemination of truth and news and humor. But who are the audiences [now]? They want relief not enlightenment. They want ease. This is fatal... The primary challenges of the theatre should not always be getting people to give a shit about it. The primary challenge should be to produce plays that reach out to people and change their lives. Theatre is not an event, like a hayride or a junior prom — it's an artistic, emotional experience in which people who have privately worked out their stories share

them with a group of people who are, without their knowledge, their friends, their peers, their equals, their partners on a remarkable ride.

The film critic David Denby shares Penn's sense that the "art" of cinema is dying and blames this on the multi-national corporatization of the business. In an article Denby wrote entitled "Has Hollywood Murdered the Movies?" for the September 14, 2012, issue of *The New Republic*, he rants against what he views as the need for the studios to play it safe and avoid offending anyone in their global audience, that has washed films of meaning. Denby's greatest ire is reserved for the *Transformers* movies which he says...

> ...are themselves based on plastic toys, in which dark whirling digital masses barge into each other or thresh their way through buildings, cities, and people, and which the moviegoer, sitting in the theater, feels as if his head were being repeatedly smashed against a wall...

Denby doesn't despise all digital fare. He praises *Avatar* and *The Avengers*. But in general he says...

> What we see in bad digital movies has the anti-Newtonian physics of a cartoon, but drawn with real figures. Rushed, jammed, broken, and overloaded, action now produces temporary sensation rather than emotion and engagement.

Denby blames all this on the studios' desire to harvest as many dollars as possible from the international marketplace, which now provides as much as two-thirds of a film's total gross. He reminds us...

> ...at the end of the year, as the Oscars loom, [the studios] distribute unadventurous but shrewdly written and played movies, such as *The Fighter,* which are made entirely by someone else. Again and again these *serioso* films win honors, but for the most part, the studios, except as distributors, don't want to get involved with them. Why not? Because they are "execution

dependent" — that is, in order to succeed, they have to be good. It has come to this: a movie studio can no longer risk making good movies. Their business model depends upon the assured audience and the blockbuster. It has done so for years and will continue to do so for years more. Nothing is going to stop the success of *The Avengers* from laying waste to the movies as an art form. The big revenues from such pictures rarely get siphoned into more adventurous projects; they get poured into the next sequel or new franchise. Pretending otherwise is sheer denial.

Denby poses the question of whether young audiences fed a strict diet of empty franchise movies will ever "...develop a taste for narrative, for character, for suspense, for acting, for irony, for wit, for drama? Isn't it possible that they will be so hooked on sensation that anything without extreme action and fantasy will just seem lifeless and dead to them?"

Denby is a smart guy, but I would argue that on a lot of levels what he wrote in this article is wrong. For one thing, the fact that the studios are selling to an international market cuts both ways. Back in the same era when I worked with Arthur Penn I was largely employed in the realm of experimental theater. One of the shows I did was *Medea*, an experiment in non-verbal communication spoken entirely in a probably made-up version of ancient Greek and Latin, directed by Andrei Serban and composed by Elizabeth Swados. We rehearsed in the black box theater in the basement of the La MaMa Experimental Theater Club with an amazing cast. A seven-year-old Diane Lane was lowered from a hole in the ceiling as the child Medea murdered. My role was to create atmosphere hitting circular saw blades with timpani mallets and to keep time on a drum while the cast chanted in these resurrected tongues.

It sounds like lunacy, but it was, in fact, a really powerful piece of theater, largely because Serban was totally clear about his intentions. The critical response to the show was spectacular, but we played for thirty-five people at a time and no one thought it would be a good idea to move to a bigger venue.

But then Ellen Stewart, La MaMa herself, decided we should take the show on the road. Our first performance was on a rainy night in Paris. The show was delayed because no one could find Ellen, and no La MaMa performance ever commenced without Ellen first putting on her false French/Cajun accent and introducing the show. When she eventually turned up she was battered and bruised. It turned out that people who had lined up to attend opening night literally hit her with their umbrellas when they were turned away from the full house. When we later moved to the international music festival in Baalbek, Lebanon, people flocked to fill the enormous Roman ruin of the Temple of Jupiter.

Serban's next production was *The Trojan Women*, also in Greek and Latin. But this time his heightened production value included the naked appearance of two women who make Megan Fox a pauper in the looks department. The show moved to Lincoln Center.

Just sayin'.

The studios didn't create American tastes. They are, however, fighting a trend that is making it increasingly difficult to sell a film. My son will trek to the theater to see *The Avengers*, but much of the rest of his entertainment comes for free on Hulu where he watches hours of Japanese anime like the show *Fooly Cooly*. The show is the product of an eccentric auteur and made by a major studio in Japan. The film begins with a mysterious girl on a motorbike slamming the hero in the head with a motorized, blue, left-handed Rickenbacker bass, an act that turns his head into a portal through which giant robots appear.

It is unlikely that this will be appearing on any major network or theater in this country — Disney could barely gather an audience for the Oscar-winning *Spirited Away*, the most beautiful and relatable of the Hayao Miyazaki anime films. There is virtually no large-scale market here for such out-of-the-box material. But those who love this stuff can now access it to their hearts' content and for free, and so the audience is drained away, niche by niche, from the theaters. People are cherry-picking the films they will pay for in the same way that iTunes has allowed them to cherry-pick songs instead of purchasing whole albums that contained one hit and a passel of filler, and that is changing the business. The studios are reacting to an increasingly picky marketplace.

So, have screenwriters been marginalized as craftsmen whose sole job is to do whatever it takes to put butts in seats rather than discovering and representing Truth, the true artist's true path? Many screenwriters and film critics look around, see the success of films like *Transformers* as a triumph of formula wrapped in high-tech effects and decorated with Megan Fox in the shortest shorts ever seen outside of porno, and say to themselves, "What's the point?" There is, of course, cause for cynicism. But especially for the newbie screenwriter, I also believe that deep immersion in this point of view is dangerous and even self-destructive.

In the first place, the idea that you can spit out hits through the application of pure formula is an urban legend. Back when I was a script reader I spent a weekend taking one of the infamous story structure workshops. The class was incredible, and by the end of the weekend I thought I understood this script guru's apparent bitterness at being relegated to the lecture circuit. He didn't have a lot that was new to say on his subject because, frankly, there isn't a lot new to say about story structure, but he said it with originality and made what we knew already coherent and replicable.

I wondered, if this guru has it figured out, why isn't he a huge writer or producer? But not long after I took that class I went to the story editor's office at Warner Bros. and I pulled my day's scripts from the stack. One of them had been submitted by this same guru. He hadn't written it, just developed it. I rushed back to my office and read his script first. But excitement turned to shock. The script was truly God-awful. I subsequently learned that ALL the scripts developed or written by this guru were on the edge of unreadable. The guy knew everything there was to know about story structure and script format. But he didn't know shit about being a writer. To the question, "Is it a movie?" this guru's products garnered a resounding, "No!"

So if structure isn't the answer, how does one codify how to deliver scripts that are actually movies?

I have two quick stories for you. Neither is rooted in the movie business, but taken together they provide a great launching platform.

The first concerns my eleven-year-old daughter who was in the throes of applying to middle schools. Her first choice was to attend the school where her two older siblings study, which for purposes of this telling we'll call Cool School. There was, of course, a lot of pressure for her to write an application essay that would help her stand out. So one night we were talking around the subject, and I noticed that she was wearing school pajama pants and that one leg was basically shredded up to her thigh. So I said, maybe it's time to get new pajamas. And she said, "Not until I get into Cool School and can buy Cool School pajamas." And it hit me: That needed to be part of her essay. "Really?" she said, but she said it with a huge grin. The notion freed her from having to be some unnaturally formal person delivering the expected essay points on "service learning" and "passion to learn" and "why I want to attend your school more than any other school." She could fulfill the needs of the essay but also have some fun by expressing herself. "By the way," she wrote, "I'm wearing torn up pajama pants and refuse to replace them until I get into your school and can buy your pajamas." And that freed her to also write something else she really believed in, "I want to go to your school because I can't wait to read every book in your library." And those two sentences — adding those bits of herself into her otherwise formulaic essay — were the reason the director of admissions read her essay and then took it out to show her colleagues. That little piece of herself made it stand out from the pack.

Here's story number two. I recently flew to New York for the final auditions of a show I'm involved with. One of the actors who came in to sing for us was a deeply talented gentleman who also happens to have enough miles on him that, as Tommy Lasorda once told me about Dodger pitcher Fernando Valenzuela's claim to be twenty-three, "His face could hold fifty years of rainwater." Those of us who had originally performed the show were not doing the new version because the producers wanted a younger cast, so this audition seemed absurd to me. I was all set to pay no attention. But when this actor started to sing I was electrified. The song he performed was "The Kid" by Buddy Mondlock. A heartbreaking rendition that began with the couplet...

> I'm the kid who ran away with the circus
> Now I'm watering elephants
> ...and ended with...
> But the truth is I could no more stop dreaming
> Than I could make them all come true

This actor didn't get the role for reasons of chemistry with the rest of the cast, but he was a pro and he understood the power of what he'd chosen to sing. Those lyrics stuck with me.

Those two couplets should be engraved over every screenwriter's desk. They embody the starting place for every successful script: a universally recognizable dilemma and a character trapped inside it. From those two very simple couplets, I know on some macro level what story I could tell. I don't have a specific picture of the character or even of the genre or time period. But I know the end points of the journey and the reason for taking it. And I can see what's universal in the idea. I have touchstones to return to throughout the writing process to ensure I am on track. I know what the theme is — what I am trying to say.

It seems worth noting that all three of the screenwriting lectures presented at a recent residency for the UC Riverside MFA program in which I teach railed against the extent to which so much of the literature about screenwriting focuses almost entirely on script structure. Screenwriting is an utterly unforgiving form that functions under the one-strike rule — miss a pivot point, go to jail, a.k.a. development hell. So it is absolutely crucial to study and learn the rules of the form. But it is not enough. There needs to be art behind the craft, a deep understanding of what your audience is hoping for mixed with a profound commitment to the Truth you want to dramatize.

Epic stakes, over-the-top villains, giant special effects — all undeniably help toward a film becoming a season's tent-pole release. But at their core, these films still depend upon the ideas the artist part of us holds precious. At the center of all these films are intimate stories and iconic images that resonate with their audience. There is, of course, a large degree of cynicism in the mix — putting Megan Fox on a motorcycle in those short-shorts springs to mind. These people are targeting a certain audience and they are shameless about how they go after that demographic.

Still, if you think it is all about spectacle and cynical manipulation, look at the comparative international box office of *Green Lantern* ($220 million) or *Cowboys & Aliens* ($175 million) versus *Transformers* ($710 million) or *The Avengers* ($1.5 billion).

So then, is it all about coming up with the right premise? The truth is, it really isn't so easy to eliminate an idea as bad, which is why as a professor I rarely steer a writer away from a premise. I mean, who would have predicted that *My Left Foot*, the true story of an Irish writer born with cerebral palsy who could control only his left foot, would be a hit? Or *Monster's Ball*, the story of a white racist who finds hope for love with a black woman? Or that the love story between two cowboys (*Brokeback Mountain*) would work as well as it did?

By and large, no matter what scale you're writing on, people connect to a film if they can find themselves somewhere in it. If the protagonist's journey is one an audience can imagine itself on, if the protagonist is living out the fantasy or fear or real life situation of its audience — and if it is told honestly — then it has a huge chance of success on its own terms. In general we care about people who are like us — flawed, filled with contradictions and trying to do the best they can. We're gentle but hiding a violent temper; we're generous but secretly resentful; we project strength but hide deep insecurities; we love but have no clue how to express that love or how to find someone who reciprocates. We want to see characters in films trying to work through those contradictions. We want to see them do that in a context that resonates with our lives and with stakes that matter to us.

What makes a great film is the same thing that makes a great story of any sort, in any form: A clearly defined journey taken by a character of clear humanity, and a clear point of view/attitude/theme, placed in a context that defines the stakes and therefore the scale of the film and helps determine how of-the-moment or relevant the film feels. As writers, what you can do is to have absolute clarity about those issues and make certain they land on your pages.

There are lots of ways to put these elements — character and premise and context — together. The writer Tod Goldberg, who is the director of the Low Residency MFA Program in Creative Writing and Writing for the Performing Arts at the University of California at Riverside, has written a short story called "Mitzvah" that he sold to television. Why did it work? It's about a hit man hiding out in Las Vegas by masquerading as a rabbi at a money-laundering temple. That combination of setting and character is so absurd — kind of like both the shrink and the mobster in *Analyze This* combined into one character — that you don't really need to know much more about the plot to imagine it as a television series. The character is the premise, the grain of sand around which to grow the plot.

But this is the exception, not the rule. Why, for example, did *The Avengers* work where *Green Lantern* did not? Why is *Lincoln* a hit when most historical dramas fail? Why is *Batman* a franchise and *Superman* a puzzle Warner Bros. has yet to solve (except maybe as a prequel)? Why did *Little Miss Sunshine* rise above the pack of indie films? Why have the latest *Sherlock Holmes* films worked when past efforts were doomed to failure?

Analyzing the success of *Transformers*

I want to look for a moment at the much maligned *Transformers*. This film is referenced most often when people describe the death of Hollywood. Is the film cynical? Of course. Is there on-the-nose dialogue? Often. Is it overblown and over-the-top? Well, I'm not sure the answer to that last question is as obvious as it might seem.

Why are the Japanese toys that form the basis for the film so pervasive? Cars and trucks are machines of immense power and destructive capability. It feels great to master them — thus the car culture — and, by the way, thus the film's early scene of our young hero being driven to buy his first car. But the dark side of the prevalence of cars becomes increasingly relevant as we pump up petroleum to pave the planet and then pump some more to power the engines that destroy our atmosphere. So the duality of the film is rooted in our real world — machines are our best friends and worst enemies.

In the trailer, we watch Sam on his way to get his first car, the universal adolescent coming-of-age ritual, and the car salesman says, "Let me tell you something, son. The driver doesn't pick the car. The car picks the driver. It's the mystical bond between man and machine." Which is, of course, what the film is all about. The obsessively detailed effects, especially as they relate to the transformations, totally bring to life the fantasy that these toys of boy power become fearsome techno-monsters that befriend, protect, need, and threaten our adolescent hero Sam. As a boy coming into his own seductive, terrifying power as an adolescent, Sam is given an iconic moment — the first time one of the robots kneels down to his level to communicate with him. This, by the way, is the same image that works so well in the much more innocent and revered *The Iron Giant* by Brad Bird and Tim McCanlies, based on the book by Ted Hughes. Our hero in that film is younger, but no less isolated by his nerdishness and broken family. Ultimately, it is the same primal idea. The writers and filmmakers were always cognizant of what the film was about and how it might attach to an audience. A *Transformers* pitch could become a lyric like the one from the Mondlock song referenced earlier:

> I'm the kid who dreamed of shagging Megan Fox
> Now I'm saving the world.
> But the truth is I could no more do it alone
> Than those giant robot things could do it without me

This of course lacks all of the poetry of the original, but the point in this case isn't to deliver poetry. It is to deliver a film that plays on certain primal forces and emotions. If that sounds more like a commercial than a film, keep in mind that the best commercials are stories as well. This one is rooted in our times, it tells an epic story, and it delivers the *über*-version of boys' fantasies that have made those toys such a huge deal. The film may be terrible in all sorts of ways, but you can take the lessons from it to the creative bank.

The Avengers versus *Green Lantern*

Both *The Avengers* and *Green Lantern* are films about superheroes recruited to save us from villainous, mythic creatures from far, far away. But *The Avengers* arrived with Joss Whedon and Zac Penn's wink; *Green Lantern* did not. More to the point, *Green Lantern* was thematically all about harnessing "the emerald energy of willpower" to defend justice across the universe, which sounds infantile and on-the-nose. At the same time, it seems to take itself very seriously given the silliness of "the emerald energy of willpower."

One would be justified in asking, why is the emerald energy of willpower dumber than "The Force" from *Star Wars*, or (God help us) *Avatar*'s "Unobtainium"? I would argue that part of the answer is that both Unobtainium and The Force steer clear of sounding like terms from a self-help manual. "The emerald energy of willpower" makes the film feel like a lecture, a haranguing, rather than an entertainment.

On the other hand, I think Unobtainium is something only a supremely confident screenwriter could even invent, let alone get away with. It is James Cameron in all his glorious arrogance telling us it's the MacGuffin and the specifics of what it is are irrelevant. It's Cameron saying, "Relax and pay attention to the good stuff." It is exactly the same as *Casablanca*'s "letters of transit," an utterly invented contrivance that carries symbolic importance and creates stakes. The fact that those letters were pointless, even absurd, did not matter one bit.

With regard to The Force: Remember, this phrase was originally used in a film that changed the world, a first that wrapped the Jungian idea of collective consciousness in the visuals of light sabers and floating spheres — and it was before the whole world was quoting Joseph Campbell. So it did not feel like the cliché it might now.

The other thing about *Green Lantern* — this is where the story about my daughter becomes relevant — there was a huge amount of it that was utterly familiar and formulaic — not in a tongue-in-cheek or an homage kind of way, but just plodding plagiarism. Watch the scene of the hero being trained by the giant alien drill sergeant. There was no spark of originality there at all. (Never mind that it also feels disturbingly racist.) It's interesting to note: The trailer for *The Avengers* looks shockingly like *Transformers,* but the originality of the writing makes it feel utterly different.

The Avengers is a superhero film that feels grounded in very current reality. The premise is that experiments in collecting clean, sustainable energy from across the universe have opened a gateway for alien creatures who want to "free us from freedom" — which is pretty much exactly what George Bush said about Bin Laden's army. The resonance of the idea that the energy we need is the energy that will kill us is obvious — Could the metaphor be any more clear? But the film's relevance to our current situation doesn't stop there. The infighting amongst the allies who could rescue us becomes the enemy of our salvation, and so plays like a riff on Washington gridlock. These both — energy and infighting — are timely topics buried in the sci-fi mythology of the story.

The writers married this premise with a band of heroes who, within the context of the kind of film it is, have real emotional relationships, real resentments, real weaknesses, and real reasons for most of them to want to avoid getting involved. Each has his or her own attitude and voice. So audience members can connect with the wish-fulfillment idea that a band of superheroes might show up to save us from the mess we have gotten ourselves into, and can also find themselves inside the very human frailties and contradictions of the heroes.

Structurally, the film is kind of interesting. *The Avengers* opens right on the inciting incident, which most books say shouldn't come until around page 15. But in *The Avengers*, the first thing that happens is that the "teseract" switches on of its own accord, opens a portal that allows the god Loki entry to our world. Loki steals the teseract, vowing to use it to allow an army of aliens to come and enslave us — and we're off collecting our flawed superheroes: Spy Natasha who has blood on her hands and a debt to pay, the brilliant Hulk with his anger management issues, squeaky-clean Captain America who is a hero out of time but maybe represents old-fashioned values we need, Thor who is locked in an eternal battle of sibling rivalry with his brother Loki, and self-obsessed Iron Man/Tony Stark who will have to learn to "play well with others" in order to lead the team to success. Each character's intro has a tone. Tony Stark, when we meet him, sees his building light up and says, "It looks like Christmas — only with more me," Whereas the Hulk comes off as depressed and reluctant.

To be fair, the film was also a genius bit of commercial manipulation on the part of Marvel. They'd whetted the audience's appetite for all these superhero characters in individual films (some more successful than others). They got to mix the tongue-in-cheek attitude of *Iron Man* with that of the more sincere (and less successful) Captain America. They got the sexiness of the Robert Downey/Gwyneth Paltrow relationship and the momentum of the *Iron Man* franchise. But I would argue that the wrong writer could have blown even all that. Writer/director Whedon found a combination of hero, villain, stakes, and superhero that had an intimate, internal, emotional journey to take that provided the audience with points of attachment.

What *The Avengers*, *Transformers*, and *Little Miss Sunshine* have in common

So here is where you can start hurling tomatoes at me: A lot of the same stuff that made *The Avengers* and *Transformers* work also allowed screenwriter Michael Arndt's *Little Miss Sunshine* to rise above the pack of that year's indies. This is a tiny film — much of it takes place inside a mini-van. The premise — a family takes to the road so a pudgy seven-year-old can compete in a beauty contest — seems quaint and burdened with minimal stakes. So why did it work?

First off, like the "family" of superheroes in *The Avengers*, the portrait of a dysfunctional family in *Little Miss Sunshine* resonates with people.

Everyone comes from some version of a dysfunctional family — and this film portrayed a doozey. There's horny, junkie grandpa. There's the pudgy, clueless, seven-year-old wannabe beauty queen. There's the miserable teenaged son who has given up speaking to everyone and only wants to fulfill his dream of becoming a pilot. There's the mom who is terrified by the state of her family but determined to hold it all together; there's the gay, suicidal uncle who is the sanest one of the bunch and the only person the son relates to. And then there is dad, the film's antagonist, who believes that any show of weakness or vulnerability is a sin and expects his family to live up to his version of perfection even as his own career swirls down the toilet.

The tensions in the film — the seven-year-old's innocence that is paired with grandpa's raunchiness, the suicidal uncle who provides solace to the desperately unhappy teenager, the pragmatic mom married to desperate dreamer dad... all this friction drives the story forward and raises what could be a tiny story to the level of comic opera in which everyone can find some piece of themselves as well as some reflection of the society we all inhabit.

Like *The Avengers* and *Transformers*, *Little Miss Sunshine* is rooted in current culture. It has a powerful message it doesn't overstate — let people be themselves. It is quirky and personal yet universal.

> I'm the kid who wanted to be a beauty queen
> Now I'm glad to have escaped with my life
> But the truth is I could no more stop dreaming
> Than I could make them all come true

Take it to the wall: *Monster's Ball*

I am increasingly convinced that a huge part of the success of these screenplays stems from the writers' clear understanding of and focus on what they were writing about. I know that probably seems like a major anti-climax, but doing the opposite is the ultimate culprit in the downfall of far too many screenplays to take the lesson for granted. These films I've been discussing put their focus on the characters and their passions, frailties, and the obstacles that force the protagonists to rise to heights beyond what seems possible. The other thing that is essential — they take their key ideas as far as they can and make them the steel core of the films. They deal with stakes that, no matter how outlandishly presented, resonate with present and real-world situations. They find voices that work for the times. At the end of the day, these are the must-have ingredients in these script's success.

Milo Addica and Will Rokos' *Monster's Ball* is maybe THE example of taking an idea and running to the edge with it, which I also believe is crucial in the success of any screenplay. Buck (Peter Boyle), Hank (Billy Bob Thornton), and Sonny (Heath Ledger) are three generations of prison guards, with the retired patriarch Hank being an unrepentant racist. In a pivotal sequence early in the film, Hank and Sonny escort a prisoner to his execution, but Sonny stumbles and throws up. Hank later slaps Sonny around for his weakness, and for "ruining" the prisoner's final moments. In the scene that follows, Sonny pulls a gun on his father and demands to know if he hates him. Hank responds, "Yeah, I hate you. I always did." And Sonny says, "Well, I always loved you," and shoots himself in the heart. It is a terrible scene to witness and utterly exemplary of the writers' commitment to their material. But look what it does. It is a confession on Hank's part of such a profound emptiness in his own soul that it allows for a film in which even a tiny ray of hope can be seen as an enormous triumph.

The place where I see so many writers sink their own premise is in stopping short of really discovering what that premise is — of not finding the core idea they are trying to expose and then running to the wall with that idea. All of your various audiences, from the agents who can sell your script to the actors who can star in the film to the audience that comes to see it — all of these people are smart and film-savvy, and the very best thing you can do to seduce all of them is to work to build a bond of trust that starts with your own scrupulous attention to your own Truth, to honesty. The audience will know if you're not in as deeply as you want it to be, and it will know if you aren't quite sure of what you want to say or of who your characters are or of what your world is like. And it will, of course, know if you are writing about stuff that has no relevance to them.

The writer Emily Rapp, my remarkable colleague at the UC Riverside program, published a piece in the November 19, 2012, issue of the online magazine *Role/Reboot* entitled, "What If This Thanksgiving Was Your Last?" This essay, like so much of what Emily writes these days, is rooted in her grief that she gave birth to a terminally ill child. Early in the piece she references an exercise she used to give writing students, which was to write about some imagined outlandish behavior around the Thanksgiving dinner table. But later in the piece she writes...

> So I'd change that writing exercise I give to students. I'd ask them instead to write a holiday dinner scene with all the people they loved best, but with the added knowledge that it will be the last time everyone sat around that table together and passed around crystal bowls full of cranberry sauce and relish dishes. Write the scene knowing that everything, always, can be fractured, broken, dissolved. Write it with the knowledge that someone around that table within the next year will drop dead, disappear, disavow. Write it knowing that the only conflict worth worrying about is this one: When faced with the choice between shutting down your emotion, at the fear of risking pain, or opening up to everything and trusting that you'll survive it, which will you choose?
>
> If you can find the beauty in that familiar dilemma that holds within it a complicated redemption, then you can find the beauty in everything, which is the task of a writer, of course, but more importantly, it is the task of a human being.

I know it's weird to say this, but on some level all of these films that work, from *Transformers* to *Monster's Ball*, heed Emily's advice. The inciting incident, the beat that launches all films, is the shattering of a life. Sometimes it's gentle, sometimes it's violent. Sometimes the references are pop culture and surfacey and sometimes they stem from profound emotions. But this shattering is always absolute — there can be no going back. And in a great screenplay, within the context of the genre, the audience's expectation of Truth is respected, characters are pushed to the ends of their endurance and then redeemed or at least understood, and the notions of the fragility of life and our need for community and hope are the driving forces.

What it all means to you

To circle back to this chapter's starting place, **if you want a career as a screenwriter you have to acquire the means to turn a great idea into a great, ready-to-package screenplay.** Really, nothing else will do.

I did promise that there is some good news in this. The fact is, by digging in you get more control of your own material. The more your screenplay actually says what you intend, the more "ready" it is to gather interested filmmakers and actors and the less chance there is that you could see your beloved project die in the terrible pits of development hell. I have been in those pits. I have even presided over some of them. Trust me, anything that keeps you from entering them is a good thing.

EXERCISES

Getting started

1. Write a few sentences describing the film you are writing or are going to write. This does not need to be a "log line" yet. Just write what you know about your protagonist and about the story you are putting him or her in.

2. Write a bit about what drew you to this subject and/or character. Please don't only write about why you think it is marketable.

3. Write about — you may not be able to do this yet — what you think is special about your treatment of this story.

4. Write a few sentences about what you think the film is about at its heart. This will morph and deepen as you write successive drafts, but it would be great to have a starting place.

5. Explain who you think the audience is for the film you want to write. Talk about why.

6. Go to Boxofficemojo.com. On the left you can click on "yearly" and then click on a year to look at the grosses for that year's films. You can start in the current year and work your way back to 1980.

   a. Analyze the way the box office has changed over the years. Are there traits that characterize the kinds of films that did well in any one year as opposed to other years?

   b. Look for how the kinds of films you are interested in writing are performing. (Note that this is not an absolute indication of how YOUR film would do. But it is an indication of how the numbers crunchers will think about financing your film.) Think about how what you've learned might define the kind of production values you can write into your film.

7. LONGER PROJECT: There are various sites on the Internet that offer free downloads of screenplays. Choose a film that you can both watch and read. Watch it, paying careful attention to why you think it either did or did not work as a film. What is it that makes you care (or not care) about the characters? About the story? About the visuals? Now go back and read the screenplay to see how much of that was actually on the page. Do this often. It's called learning to watch films and read scripts like a writer.

2

WHAT DRIVES A FILM:

A preparatory look under the hood

There are lots of ways to define a film. Director/producer Sydney Pollack has been quoted as saying that a great film is a compelling story interrupted by the plot. He meant that the protagonist needs to be interesting and involved in his/her life BEFORE the plot of the film kicks in to interrupt. What is the plot? Steve Almond, in his self-published *This Won't Take But a Minute, Honey*, tells us, "Plot is the mechanism by which your protagonist is forced up against her deepest fears and/or desires." (p.23)

Here, in the most general terms, is what makes a screenplay: A (usually) flawed character is introduced living his or her life. Oftentimes he/she is in the middle of some transaction — something is about to happen. But then something unexpected occurs (called the inciting incident) that completely detonates that life. The inciting incident is like a black box. Your protagonist goes in wanting one thing and comes out wanting something entirely different. It is his/her drive to get what he/she wants against all odds that powers the rest of the film.

The plot of a film will usually place your protagonist on three separate but interlocking journeys:

(a) The external journey to get what they want.

(b) The internal journey of reconciling their internal

contradiction, of coming to grips with the difference between what they want and what they need.

(c) The key emotional journey. Sometimes this is a standard love story, but that is far from always the case. In *Amadeus* it is the story of a composer scorned — by God. In *The Fugitive* it is the growing relationship between fugitive Kimble and U.S. Marshal Gerard. In *The King's Speech* it is the dawning of a friendship between the future King of England and his speech therapist.

In bundling these journeys together into a story for film, there are very specific bits of information and plot beats you have to provide for your audience. Exactly when you reveal these beats — screenplay structure — is presented by many script gurus as absolutely rigid. It is absolutely not, though assuming that rigidity can be useful when you are first learning the craft. But ultimately, the point is to absorb and execute on the essence of the rules of screenwriting craft, not to hit a particular beat at a specific page or word-count.

Most of the literature on screenwriting divides scripts into three acts. A script for a feature film generally (although there are exceptions) ranges from 90 to 120 pages in length, assuming it is in standard screenplay format. The most reliable template for format is what's called Warner format, named for the wonderful Warner Bros. Script Processing Department that codified it. Every draft of every screenplay developed at Warner Bros. is run through Script Processing. The reasons are twofold: Executives can easily tell when writers ordered to trim their scripts have accomplished the required page reductions simply by altering their margins. And through some act of magic, a page of script formatted by Warner Script Processing times out to a minute a page, so executives and producers have immediate script timings.

In most discussions of structure, scripts are roughly broken into quarters. Act One usually comprises the first quarter. Act Two spans the middle two quarters. Act Three is usually the final quarter. I say usually because there are variations. A long Act One is usually (but not always) a bad idea because in general, especially in these times when patience is in short supply, you want to get to Act Two — the point where the plot really kicks in — as quickly as possible. Similarly, sometimes the climax of a film can be over fairly quickly and sometimes it takes a little longer than usual.

Each act has a really specific function. In general...

Act One, which with the rare exception should comprise no more than the first quarter of your script, is when your main characters, plots, and subplots are set into motion. Genre, tone, voice, time, place, rhythm, and theme are established. If there is a secret to be revealed later in the script — and most great scripts have one — that secret is established in Act One. We learn who the characters are, what their lives look like before the plot really kicks into gear. The act always includes or implies a moment that spins your protagonist's life in a new direction and introduces a new, must-have something or someone that the protagonist wants. The act ends when an unexpected and somehow perilous opportunity for your protagonist to pursue that want opens up. The decision to take that opportunity is the start of...

Act Two: The section that most people call Act Two is approximately the length of half the script and is broken into halves separated by what is cleverly called "the midpoint." I actually believe it is useful to think of Act Two as two separate acts, broken up at the midpoint where the action is once again spun around in a new direction. I'm going to call these subsections Act 2a and Act 2b so as not to add to the confusion by having to name a fourth act.

In Act 2a, things seem to go fairly well for your protagonist. The antagonist, who is introduced in Act One or at the latest in the beginning of Act Two and is the person or (rarely) thing that works to prevent your protagonist from getting what he/she wants, is certainly present in the story. But success still seems to be within your protagonist's reach. This section ends at the midpoint when the protagonist makes a discovery or has an encounter that once again spins the story in a new direction. The midpoint involves a change in direction for the protagonist and/or the antagonist so that their vectors begin to approach one another in Act 2b more than they did in 2a.

Act 2b is where you get to put on the black leather and really torture the protagonist you love along his/her way to getting (or not getting) what he/she wants. Things don't go so well for the protagonist in this part of the script. Stakes heighten; obstacles get increasingly more daunting. More and more is required of your protagonist because his or her flaws become increasingly pronounced or relevant, and because your antagonist turns out to be much more clever and persistent than your protagonist could have ever imagined. The act builds to a place where your protagonist's chances for success appear to be close to zero — this is called "the low point." The act ends with the second plot point, the presentation of one final, desperate, do-or-die opportunity for the protagonist to accomplish his/her goal.

Act Three: The final quarter of the script is where your protagonist gets to execute on a final plan, to take one last shot at getting what he/she wants. The stakes are usually do-or-die, by which I mean that either your protagonist will get what he/she wants or lose the opportunity to ever try for it again. There is a final pivot point, the climax of the movie, where all will be decided. And then a bit of an epilogue to give us a taste of what his or her new life will look like.

What is a scene?

A scene usually runs three pages or less in length, because more than three minutes in any one location and on any one subject typically starts to feel stagnant. The purpose of a scene, except in a comedy where scenes can exist purely to be funny, is to move the story forward in a dramatic context. A scene has a beginning, middle, and end. Your goal is usually to get into a scene as late as possible and out as early as possible.

A scene without dramatic tension isn't really a scene. That is, two characters just talking at one another, or a character talking purely for the purpose of delivering exposition, is not a scene. In an article called "Whose Afraid of Nichols and May?" written by Sam Kashner about the brilliant comedy team of Mike Nichols and Elaine May for the January, 2013, issue of *Vanity Fair*, Nichols says to May, "...we figured out over a long time that there were only three kinds of scenes in the world — fights, seductions, and negotiations." (p.98) The protagonist of a scene always has an agenda and always faces obstacles to that agenda. This push toward an objective is what energizes a scene.

A scene has a shape, a kind of musical dynamic that moves either from high to low or low to high. Maybe a character enters a scene as an underdog but wins the fight. Or, a woman can enter a scene thinking she's all that, confident she can easily win the heart of the guy, only to discover that the guy's heart is already spoken for. Or, a character can come into a scene hoping to learn something but discover something altogether different. Each example either exceeds or disappoints expectations.

Scenes that bundle together to carry the film from one major story point to the next are called sequences. Like a scene, a sequence has a shape and a dynamic, either moving a character closer or further from his/her goal. They never — or almost never — leave a character in the same place he/she was at the beginning of the sequence.

The rhythm of reverses

The flow of scenes, one to the next, is as important in screenwriting as the flow of notes is to composing. The words that need to be engraved over your writing desk are "reverses" and "consequences." *South Park* writers Matt Stone and Trey Parker gave a talk as part of a series filmed for MTV in which they explained that every scene (and, I would add, every sequence of scenes) in a storyline must be connected either by "BUT THEN..." or "THEREFORE...." In each storyline, every scene or sequence must either compel the one that follows or reverse the motion of its predecessor. Scenes or sequences connected instead by "and then" are death as there is no energy in the connection, no push from one to the next. What you are looking for is a captivating rhythm of consequences and reverses, the stuff that will allow your film editor and composer to lock onto the perfect groove for your film.

Look, for example, at the macro-structure just presented of the acts and their pivot points:

- In Act One you establish your protagonist in his/her normal life. By and large, things are running at a smooth clip.

- BUT THEN the inciting incident interrupts that flow entirely. Nothing can ever be the same. The protagonist has something or someone new he/she has to have. THEREFORE his/her life is in turmoil.

- BUT THEN the first plot point provides a unique opportunity to pursue that want. It is dangerous, but the want is strong. THEREFORE, after a beat of hesitation he/she decides to take that opportunity. The antagonist tries to stop forward motion, but things go okay for the protagonist, who moves forward in his/her journey.

- BUT THEN we hit the midpoint and something occurs to reverse that. The antagonist starts to close in, or the protagonist is forced onto a new and more dangerous road, or the protagonist's failings really kick in, or something is revealed. THEREFORE, by the end of Act Two — the low point — things look utterly hopeless for the protagonist.

- BUT THEN one more, nearly impossible opportunity presents itself. The protagonist knows by this point that, either literally or figuratively, he/she can't live without achieving the goal set up in Act One. THEREFORE he/she goes for it, driving the film through the climax and into the portrait of life after this journey...

This is the way you need to think on every level of the film, all the way down to the level of scenes that also need to have a beginning, middle, and end, dramatic tension, and reverses. A man goes into a scene hoping to talk to the woman of his dreams but discovers that his mouth has become disconnected from his brain. Or, a woman goes into a courtroom scene to prove her husband a monster but instead winds up painted as an incompetent mother. As we move into structuring your screenplay, it is vital to keep this rhythm in mind.

Character creation — a quick primer

We will also study at length how one creates compelling characters, but there are a couple of thoughts I want you to hold close as we enter the body of this book.

1. There are two primary dialectics that are the keys to great film characters — and therefore to great films. (These tensions are also often the basis for generating a compelling log line.) The more recognizable these tensions are, the more likely your film will connect with an audience. To whatever extent possible, you want to construct a character who in certain key ways could not be less suited to the journey ahead. These broad-strokes characteristics may seem like simplified versions of character work, but in fact are often all you need.

   a. Want versus need: Think, for example, of Luke Skywalker in the original *Star Wars* film. Luke wanted to become a Jedi Warrior, but needed first to learn to trust himself and his connection to The Force. Many a film derives its energy from the journey the protagonist takes to realize that what he/she needs is not necessarily the same as what he/she wants.

   b. Character contradiction. This is sometimes, but not always, the same as the want/need dialectic. Think of how much mileage *The Fugitive* gets from the tension between Dr. Richard Kimble's desire to stay out of the hands of the law versus his unshakeable compunction to stop and help everyone in need no matter how much it puts his freedom or life at risk. In this case it is Kimble's loyalty to both of these characteristics that ultimately saves his life. Or think about *Amadeus*, in which the primary engine of the film is the terrible reality that Antonio Salieri yearns to be the greatest living composer but is blessed only with the ability to recognize true genius when he hears it. Or Butch Cassidy, who is an honorable man but an incorrigible thief. These contradictions between competing strands in our characters' personalities are enormously powerful tools to both drive your story and to establish your characters' humanity, the key to building close relationships with your readers and audience.

2. A film is as good as its antagonist. Again, we will get into this in greater depth later, but in your initial planning for your film sadism is really important. The rhythm of reverses must build in a pattern of escalating stakes. The forces of antagonism in your screenplay must, within the context of the genre and nature of your screenplay, push your protagonist right up to his/her breaking point. Anything less will be dull.

The process for moving forward

Not everything mentioned above will be clear to you when you start your script. Sometimes your theme will not be obvious until you finish a draft. Sometimes your protagonist will betray you and take second fiddle to some other character. The fact that your piece may remain molten through a number of drafts is no cause to abandon the attempt to lock down as much as you can before you start to write. My own process is to write what I can of an outline, including all the major pivot points, before starting and then fill in the blanks and revise as the work progresses. This applies to first drafts.

Once you have a draft you should absolutely lock in a complete outline before you start your revision. But that is a topic for later.

Over the next four chapters, I am going to try to walk you through the construction of an outline and character bible. Each of those chapters will end with exercises designed to leave you with a blueprint for your film. The trick will be to avoid getting hung up if there is a point you don't know yet. Move at the pace that works for you.

Different writers use different techniques to assemble their outlines. The traditional method is to use note cards, with different colors representing different plotlines. The advantage of this is that it allows easy shuffling or replacing of scenes. But there are other ways. Most screenwriting programs have a note card function, though I find those restrictive because of the number of cards you can see at once. I also sometimes use a program designed for building organization charts and meeting agendas. It is important to find the method that resonates best with the way your mind works — that allows you to start to visualize how your script will lay out.

EXERCISES

Nailing down the basics

1. Choose one of the films you watched for the exercises in the previous chapter. You may need to watch/read it again. Fill in this paragraph:

   (Name of the protagonist) is living his or her life as (please describe). _____ is about to happen when _____ occurs that makes going back to that life impossible. After that, all he/she can think of, all he or she wants, is _____. But (name the antagonist) tries everything he/she can to prevent the protagonist from getting what he/she wants. Not only that — the protagonist is really unprepared for this journey and this antagonist because _____. Ultimately, the protagonist (uncovers a secret? has a revelation about him or herself? solves a mystery? all of the above?) that enables him or her to make one final attempt to get what he or she wants. In the end, _____ happens.

2. Regarding the same film, describe...

   a. The external journey of the protagonist: What does he or she want? What does he or she need to go through to get it?

b. The protagonist's internal journey: What does the protagonist learn about him or herself? Another way of asking this is, try to describe the difference between what the character wants and what the character needs.

c. The emotional story: One way or the other, there will be a story of emotional connection (or disconnection) in the film. With whom does that happen? Describe that story.

3. Look at a particular section of the plot, say ten minutes and/or ten pages. Describe the rhythm of reverses by laying out a series of scenes and indicate (a) which is high energy and which is low energy; (b) which has a positive outcome for the protagonist and which don't go so well for him/her.

4. Assemble your materials for the work to come. If you want to outline on note cards, make sure you have a supply of them in various colors. A corkboard and pushpins are handy, but not absolutely necessary for this method. Have a notebook and dividers for your character bible.

ACT ONE – STRUCTURE:
Lessons from the near-death of *The Fugitive*

Strap in, because these next two chapters on the first thirty pages/ Act One are going to be long. Why?

- Because the vital character traits, wants and needs, theme, genre, tone, and rhythm are all established in Act One.

- Because all of the momentum your script will ever have derives from how you launch your story.

- Because the first thirty pages are when you hook your reader.

- And because if you get into trouble as you develop your screenplay the issues can more often than not be traced to the opening act. Get your Act One right and you can save yourself a tremendous amount of grief later on.

My first job in Hollywood was reading screenplays for a producer who paid me mini-money to cover thirty pages of a script and tell him whether it was worth paying someone more experienced to read the whole thing. I used to laugh a lot about that gig, but over the years I have come to really understand the thirty-page rule: If the first thirty pages aren't working, the script won't either. This producer didn't have the wherewithal to finance draft after draft trying to get a workable script out of some premise he liked but that was buried in a bad draft. So what sounded ridiculous on first hearing was in fact pretty smart. Fail in the first thirty pages and you won't sell your script. It's that simple.

When I worked at Warner Bros., I had the great fortune to work with the film editor Dede Allen, whose extraordinary career included *Dog Day Afternoon*, *Serpico*, *Little Big Man*, *Bonnie and Clyde*, *Wonder Boys*, *The Addams Family*, *The Breakfast Club*, and *The Wiz*. Dede had been brought into the studio to advise the production executives during post production. I had the opportunity to spend weeks in the cutting room with her, and she taught me one of the most valuable lessons I ever learned about story: If you have a problem in reel six, don't re-cut reel six. Go back and look at reel one.

This was a revelation that I have found to be almost universally useful in script development. **If a screenplay loses steam in the second or third acts, more often than not it is because the script was not set up or thought out properly in Act One.** The converse is also usually true: If the first thirty pages of a script are not working, there is almost no chance the script as a whole will work. So Act One is where I spend a lot of my time working with writers. It is the territory that contains the most cleverly disguised, far-too-easy-to-fall-through trapdoors into Development Hell.

Act One story points

Please note that I am not going to lay out specific pages where certain beats are to occur. There are all kinds of variations on the order and placement of what I am going to describe. But at the end of the day, all first acts need to accomplish the same things and hit the same basic beats...

- Portrait of the protagonist's EVERYDAY LIFE before the plot kicks in: What you want in this section is to establish your protagonist in the middle of his/her life. We learn a bit about who he/she is and what he/she values. A story is usually put into motion that will then be interrupted. This is where you create the world of safety that will be forever yanked away at the...

- INCITING INCIDENT: The inciting incident is the Sydney Pollack moment when the plot interrupts the story of everyday life. Historically, there are two kinds of inciting incidents. In old-fashioned hero stories we meet a person or community of some sort, something happens to endanger that person or community, and the near-perfect hero rides in to save the day. In the other version, which exists in 99% of modern films, the inciting incident is the moment when your protagonist's everyday life is detonated. (Part of the genius of *The Avengers* is that it is both: The world is threatened and a team of imperfect heroes' lives are interrupted when they are summoned to rescue us.) Think of Act One as the deck of a demented aircraft carrier. Your protagonist is in his/her jet, monitoring the everyday prep for that day's very ordinary mission. The inciting incident is a catapult that somehow launches this person at the shockingly wrong moment, upside-down and spinning out of control, just before the carrier explodes. What I want to emphasize is the violence of the moment. Within the context of the kind of story you are telling, the moment needs to be cataclysmic. Out of this moment is born the new thing that your protagonist HAS TO HAVE, the thing he/she will WANT and chase for the rest of the film. In order for your film to work, this want has to be desperate, and it has to be CLEAR. Again within the context of the story you are telling, it needs to be life and death. It can be the death of the protagonist's son or it can be meeting the woman of your protagonist's dreams, or anything in between.

- FIRST PLOT POINT: So your protagonist is out there in his/her jet, completely disoriented. Someone has blown up the carrier (everyday life), so there is no going back. There is exactly one point on the horizon that might provide salvation if your protagonist can just get there. She discovers one daring maneuver that might allow her to pull out of the tailspin and chase that point — though there is nothing but flak between where she is and where she's headed. The maneuver is dangerous, the journey ahead fraught, so even though the situation is dire the decision to make the move is not a simple one. The moment when your protagonist recognizes that opportunity is called the first plot point. The moment of decision that follows the few beats of hesitation necessary to communicate to the audience how profound this moment is, is the start of Act Two.

Those are the major Act One pivot points: everyday life, inciting incident, first plot point, and the decision to move ahead. But there is much more that is set up and communicated in these pages.

- GENRE: Comedy, drama, thriller, action — these all (and their combinations) set up certain expectations for your audience. You need to establish that up front. A comedy needs to give the audience permission to laugh; an action film needs to plant an action sequence early in the film; etc. For the most part — though there are counter-examples — the rest of the script needs to remain consistent with what you establish.

- TONE: This is, of course, related to genre. How dark or funny or witty or romantic do you want the piece to be? Is it lyrical or staccato?

- THEME: Most of the time the theme of your piece will be stated someplace in Act One. Eventually it will be terribly important to be able to succinctly state what your film is about, though you may not know precisely what that is until you have finished your draft and your characters have taken over and made the film their own. Once you have the theme, every scene, every move your protagonist makes can be judged according to whether that scene speaks to it.

- SECRET AT THE HEART OF THE FILM: This can be the fact that the protagonist we have been following is really a ghost, or it can be the protagonist's discovery that the treasure she's been hunting has really been under foot the entire time, or it can be the revelation that the antagonist is really the protagonist's father, etc. The point is, most films rely on some late Act Two revelation to send the protagonist on the final leg of his/her journey, and that revelation cannot come from out of left field. It needs to be set up or hinted at in Act One, and then clues must be embedded in the rest of the film so that the revelation doesn't seem like just some new bit of information dropped into the film at the last minute. What you never want to do is reveal something late in the film with no antecedents. M. Night Shyamalan's *The Sixth Sense* only works because when it is revealed that the protagonist has actually been dead for nearly the entire film, the audience can replay the movie and discover the hints that had been implanted.

• PERIOD AND LOCALE: What is the time period and locale of the story? In what way are those elements important? Do either become a character in your story?

• What is the TIME FRAME of your story? In other words, over what period of time does it occur? Will the seasons be important?

Analysis: Act One of *The Fugitive*

I use a couple of films as examples in this book. One is *The Fugitive*, written by Jeb Stuart and David Twohy and directed by Andrew Davis. *The Fugitive* was the first major film I ever worked on and so I know a lot of its history. But, more than that, I reference *The Fugitive* because, although it was made twenty years ago, in many ways it remains one of the best examples of Hollywood filmmaking that I know.

One note before I begin: The process a script goes through from the writer's submission draft to the screen is often maligned as a torturous and destructive folly. But sometimes that collaboration can create magic. David Twohy's draft had many of the big set pieces that remained in the film as great examples of showing character through action. But in other respects the script changed a lot through collaboration. The entire structure of the first act was flipped on its head by director Andrew Davis and his team of editors in post production. Before Andy came on board, Twohy's draft had the mysterious antogonist (the "one-armed man") turn out to be in the employ of Marshal Gerard, an idea that turned out to be much too complicated. So when Andy became the director, he asked his sister, who was a nurse, to discuss with her colleagues how a doctor could be framed. She came back with the idea that Kimble should be threatening to denounce as dangerous a new drug which was being tested, thus prompting the pharmaceutical company to try to frame him for murder. Thus was born the whole Devlin-MacGregor subplot that became the foundation on which the film was built.

What I want you to notice as we go through Act One is how the script's first act does its job with elegance, simplicity, and clarity.

- EVERYDAY LIFE: Dr. Richard Kimble arrives late to a benefit. He is introduced as a successful and charming doctor with a beautiful wife and a happy marriage. His objective is to collect his wife and get out of there. Social obligations stand in his way. This scene is actually a series of mini-seductions as Kimble works the room. Kimble's best friend Dr. Lentz returns the keys to Kimble's car and thanks him for the loan, then introduces Kimble to an executive from drug company Devlin-MacGregor. "This is the doctor I've been telling you about," says Lentz of Kimble. The executive's look tells us he's not thrilled by what he's heard about Kimble. Both beats plant the film's CENTRAL SECRET, offering hints that the audience can play back when it is later revealed that Lentz ordered the hit that will leave Kimble's wife dead. At the benefit, Kimble rescues his wife from the conversation she is trapped in and they head home. There is clearly some bed-action in the cards... BUT THEN...

- Kimble gets called to assist in a surgery. Kimble's wife promises to wait up. We are at that point eager to see how that story plays out...

- Surgery — we learn that Lentz was supposed to do this surgery but can't be found, another hint to pick up later.

- INCITING INCIDENT: Kimble returns home ready to continue where he left off in the car BUT THEN discovers that his wife has been murdered. He struggles with the one-armed killer. (This also helps establish genre.) BUT THEN...

- NEW WANT ESTABLISHED: Kimble is accused and convicted of his wife's murder. Clearly, "normal life" is over — Kimble tells us as much when he says of the killer, "He took everything." But also, Kimble clearly states what he wants when he says to the cop who accuses him, "You find that man," meaning the one-armed man who Kimble swears is the real killer.

- FIRST PLOT POINT: Convicted, Kimble is THEREFORE put onto a prison bus for incarceration and execution. BUT THEN prisoners attempt an escape that goes wrong. THEREFORE, the bus crashes. Kimble is the only person to remain behind to save the life of one of his jailors before leaping to safety. The bus crash is the first plot point, the moment that provides Kimble with the opportunity to escape and pursue the killer on his own. (Note: This is also the first of several amazing scenes in which action establishes character and character enriches action. One of Kimble's defining traits is that he is compelled at every turn to do the right thing by people no matter how dangerous that is for him. Kimble very nearly dies saving the life of his jailor, which tells us a huge amount about his character. And the fact that we love him for that makes us all the more invested in the action sequence.)

- THEME STATED: Right before Kimble flees he has an encounter with the worst of the prisoners. As they part, Kimble says, "Be good." It is spoken with irony but it is also the theme of the piece — Richard Kimble triumphs in the end by persuading his antagonist to trust him, and he does that in large part by confounding expectations and always doing right by the people he encounters.

- BEGINNING OF ACT TWO: Richard Kimble hesitates for just a beat but finally takes advantage of the opportunity provided by the crash, flees into the woods, and we are off into Act Two.

One of the things that is so interesting about *The Fugitive* is that the film differs from the screenplay in a fundamental way. While the script had a traditional Act One structure as outlined above, the film flipped that structure on its head and opened on the inciting incident — the death of Dr. Richard Kimble's wife — and then filled in "everyday life" through flashback. It was a brilliant restructuring that pulled the audience right into the film but still allowed it to hit all of its structural milestones. There are other films that have done this flip since. *Run Lola Run* and *The Avengers* both open on the inciting incident. I will discuss both films in greater detail later. For now, the point is that if you know the rules you can bend them so long as you hit the vital points.

A tale from the trenches: What the studio didn't understand about *The Fugitive* and how it nearly killed the film

The on-set revelation that the key to this film would be constant momentum found one of its key expressions early in post. David Twohy and Jeb Stuart, under director Andy Davis' tutelage, had concocted a brilliant Act One. As already discussed, Andy and his editing team re-structured that part of the film, opening the film on the murder of Kimble's wife (the inciting incident) to energize the film and set the tone from the outset. It was a great decision. The power of a great Act One was never so evident than it was at *The Fugitive*'s first preview, which by the way happened so impossibly soon after the end of production that it forever changed post-production schedules.

At that preview, the audience leapt to its feet after the bus crash sequence as though it was live theater. The film owned the audience from there out. The market research scores were so off-the-charts that at the after-screening party the usually fierce and taciturn studio boss Bob Daly giddily threw his arms around me — and I promise you, at that point in my career he had no clue at all who I was or what I'd done on the film.

He also didn't know that we'd very nearly blown it.

At some point when we were developing the script, even though we had this great Act One that established a kinetic pace and brilliantly defined Richard's Kimble's character through action, the entire cast of executives on the project — there were three of us, with me being the junior — became obsessed with the idea that we needed to find a moment when Kimble could stop running so we could focus on learning about his state of mind. We played with a sequence of scenes in which Julianne Moore's doctor character took Kimble home, and — when that didn't work — with a sequence in which Kimble spent the night with a waitress. None of this ever seemed to fit, but we kept noodling it.

It was only after the start of production that executive Bob Brassel phoned me from location to say they had dropped the sequence. Somehow, the group that was continuing to develop the script — Bob, writer Jeb Stuart, director Andrew Davis, producer Peter Macgregor-Scott, and stars Harrison Ford and Tommy Lee Jones — figured out why the sequence never seemed to fit: It was wildly inappropriate and totally unnecessary. The revelation was that the script delivered so much character through action that Andy needed to shoot and cut a film defined by constant momentum. Halting that movement so that Kimble could reflect on what had happened to him would have contradicted what had been set up in Act One. Also, of course, Richard Kimble was still in mourning for his wife and intimacy with some other woman was out of the question. The idea that had so captivated us as executives turned out to have been utterly wrongheaded. Consistency to what was established in Act One was key.

Why did Act One of *The Fugitive* work so well? Well, because the writer and filmmakers were absolutely clear about what they needed to accomplish. They knew what character traits and themes to bring to the forefront and they were willing to pare back everything else. And they hit all their marks, even if in the film they did so "out of order." Although work continued on Act Three throughout production, the writers had set themselves the solidest of foundations and given their audience easy access to the story and characters that would hook them.

EXERCISES

Act One structure/begin your outline

1. For the project you are working on, write a paragraph response to each of these questions:
   a. What defines your protagonist's life before the inciting incident? What is most valuable to him/her? What is it about that life that might be valuable as he/she moves through the story?
   b. What is the inciting incident? In what way does it change your protagonist's life? What does he/she want as a result of it? What happens to her or him if she/he doesn't get it?
   c. What is the first plot point? What is the opportunity that is opened up as a result? What is it about this opportunity that seems dangerous or difficult?

2. Turn shortened versions of the answers to a, b, and c above into bullet points. This will be the starting place for your outline.

3. Write out the answers to the following. These should be living paragraphs that develop as you write.
   a. What is your theme? (This might not be clear yet.)
   b. What is the secret at the heart of the film?
   c. What is the genre and tone of the film?
   d. What is the time period and locale of the story? In what way are those elements important?

e. What is the time frame of your story? In other words, over what period of time does it occur? Will the seasons be important?

f. What does your protagonist need? What are his/her flaws that will stand in the way of getting what he/she wants? In other words, in what way(s) is he/she unsuitable for the journey ahead?

g. What is at stake? What happens to your protagonist if he/she does not get what he/she wants after the inciting incident?

4. Refine your image of your target audience. Who do you expect will want to see your film?

4 A DEEPER DIVE INTO ACT ONE:
Creating great characters

Setting up your protagonist/
Creating castable roles

It should go without saying that one of the things people read for is whether or not the roles in a screenplay are castable. This should be important to the writer as well. Scripts rarely succeed based on pyrotechnics or setting alone. On a purely artistic level, more often than not great characters make for great screenplays. On a more pragmatic level you want to attract the best actors possible to bring your story to life. And depending on the size of the venture, you may need the help of some star power to get your project financed. Finally, great "actor candy" roles are defined by the burdens the character carries, the flaws they overcome, and the journeys they embark upon — exactly the same traits that will draw in an audience.

I'm going to write here about your protagonists, but understand that most of what I say applies to varying degrees to all of your characters.

Your goal in Act One, put as simply as possible, is to create a character who will drive all of the major action of your film but who in certain fundamental ways could not be more ill-equipped for the journey you are going to send him/her on. In creating him/her, you need to obsess over him/her, to fall in love no matter what the flaw. You have to know everything about him or her. You have to feel compassion for his or her flaws. You have to know why he or she is doing everything, saying everything, feeling everything. You will know your writing is on the right track when your protagonist is whispering in your ear day and night like some demented lover.

The irony, of course, is that in order for your screenplay to work you have to be willing in Act Two to torment and frustrate this "lover" you created to within a centimeter of his or her sanity. You have to drive your protagonist to the edge of reason, to a frustration so profound that only the most desperate act can save them. But this is the task of Act Two, and we're not there yet. Your protagonist needs to be constructed before the torture can begin.

Great characters carry a burden for us. They are iconic in that they represent some journey we have taken or want to take or fear taking. They have frailties we recognize, and we root for them to overcome those frailties to get what they want because we root for ourselves to overcome them, and because what they want somehow resonates for us. With rare exceptions, audiences have little interest in perfect characters because they are unrecognizable — they are not "human." (This, BTW, is part of what makes the *Superman* franchise so tough to crack.) It is a character's frailties and uncertainties that make even the most unlikely characters universal.

As an example, Edward in *Edward Scissorhands* was an unfinished robot made to look human but for the blades that stood in for hands. He was an utterly bizarre creation, but he was also plagued by a staple of the human condition — isolation and loneliness. Audiences recognized that and so identified with his plight.

Character contradiction

To be a great screenwriter is to embrace a process of compassionate sadism. You have to create a protagonist you love and then set him or her on a journey for which he or she could not be less suited. You are looking to give him/her a "want" that both his nature and his situation make nearly impossible to achieve. The sadism actually starts in Act One because in creating your protagonists you need to imbue him/her with characteristics that make him/her the least suitable candidate for the journey of the film. You want to make the external journey your protagonist takes as difficult as possible and, unless you are creating a pure hero, to give them the greatest distance possible to travel internally.

The gods, or the muses, or whatever it is that helps us in our writing, offered me an ah-ha moment as I was struggling to find a way to express this. I had been fascinated for some time by the phenomenon that is Tim Burton. Here is a guy whose sensibility is as eccentric as can be and yet he is a billion-dollar filmmaker. How is that possible? So when the Los Angeles County Museum opened an exhibit of Tim's art, I went to see it, trolling for answers.

The first thing that struck me was that amidst all the weirdness there were a few portfolio pages from his life drawing classes at the California Institute for the Arts. Tim had studied and mastered traditional art before he departed into his own universe. In other words, don't be fooled by the eccentricity. Don't let it mask the fact that he worked his ass off to learn his craft.

I don't know why this took me by surprise. In both my musician and filmmaking careers I had noticed that, no matter what I thought of the end product, an artist's success implied mastery — often obsessive mastery — of the craft they were engaged in. But screenwriting has some odd baggage to overcome. I once heard script guru Robert McKee say, "No one who goes to jazz clubs for twenty years suddenly decides they can play the saxophone. But for some reason people who go to the movies for a few years think they can write films." Tim Burton was a reminder that this could not be further from the truth.

But I digress. The other, more profound discovery at the museum was a page of notes Burton had written about the character of Edward Scissorhands. At the bottom of the page he'd scribbled, "Hobbies: Carving ice sculptures."

Okay, does that feel anti-climactic? Pay attention: It was Tim's recognition of the vital importance of character contradiction that struck me. What that note said was that in creating this film Tim felt he needed to understand everything about his character, down to his hobbies — and his choice of hobbies was deeply embedded in character.

Here was this extraordinary creation, a human-looking robot but for his unfinished hands, a freak with deadly weapons at the end of his arms — and his hobby was sculpting ice! It was a pragmatic, witty, gentle and cinematic choice for a visual cue to Edward's fundamental contradiction: *He looks like a monster — but is, in fact, profoundly human.*

It is not possible to overstate the importance of discovering the defining contradictions and dramatizing them for us. The two sides of these character contradictions are in fact the elements that combine and combust inside a film's engine to drive your story forward. Although you want to know the fine details and subtleties of your protagonist's life, discovering the broad strokes that describes the character's defining contradictions is essential to making your script sing.

Screenwriter William Goldman tells a great story about the character of Butch Cassidy:

> One of the great true Cassidy stories was when he was young and in jail in Wyoming, I think it was, and he came up for parole and the Governor met with him and said, "I'll parole you if you'll promise to go straight." And Butch thought a moment and then said this: "I can't do that." In the stunned silence he went on, "But I'll make a deal with you — if you'll let me out, I promise never to work in Wyoming again."
>
> And the governor took the deal.
>
> And Butch never robbed in Wyoming again.
>
> Even today, that's probably the best character introduction I ever came across... that kind of building block is essential when you're stumbling through material, trying to get a grip on the best way to tell this particular story. The entire Superposse chase, almost a half an hour of screen time, was only writable for me because I knew the Sundance Kid couldn't swim..."[1]

Notice, please, how specific these two traits are and yet how broadly defining. Butch had outlaw in his DNA, but he was also utterly

[1] Goldman, William. *Four Screenplays With Essays — Marathon Man, Butch Cassidy and the Sundance Kid, The Princess Bride, and Misery.* Applause Books, 1995. Pages 2-3.

honorable — what a GREAT character contradiction. Sundance outran the posse to a place where there was only one escape — and fearless Sundance was terrified, not by the leap from the cliff, but by the fact that he couldn't swim.

Notice, too, that the traits Goldman latches onto determine action. Which is to say, they are filmable. So, so, so important. And they are quirky — fascinating — fun — tragic — compelling... Goldman goes on to say,

> Anyway, I've got this wondrous Governor anecdote.
>
> And it fell out of the movie... The movie I wrote was about these two legends who become legends all over again in a different country. I had no time to get Butch arrested, jailed, and then offered a pardon. And no governor with a sniff at re-election is going to release the most famous outlaw of his time... Faulkner said one of the great things, "In writing you must kill all your darlings." I'm not sure I totally subscribe to that but I do believe this: you damn well better be willing to.
>
> The Governor story was not wasted, of course. It was absolutely the foundation for the character of Butch. But it could not appear in the film — it didn't fit. Several of you are facing this obstacle, having written stuff that you love but that doesn't really serve your story. Toughen up, get out the cleaver, thin the herd of great ideas when you must. Your writing will be infinitely better for it.[2]

Here are some other examples:

In *The Fugitive*, Dr. Richard Kimble needs to stay a step ahead of the U.S. Marshal who is pursuing him, but Kimble is also compelled in any given situation to follow his instincts to help people. Marshal Sam Gerard is rigid in his refusal to consider the guilt or innocence of the fugitives he pursues but the very instincts that make him a great hunter mean he can't ignore the humanity behind Kimble's behavior. This sets up the chase between an implacable hunter and a man who we know deserves the support of the man sworn to uphold the law.

---

2 Ibid. Page 3.

James Cameron's *Avatar* is a film with astounding visuals and captivating creatures. But I would argue that the thing that makes it work so well for audiences is this contradiction: In his quest to be a hero, warrior Jake Sully makes a deal with the devil to regain the use of his legs but discovers he has the heart of an angel. This is a classic template that also is at the heart of films like *The Man Who Would Be King* and *Dances With Wolves*. This contradiction is hinted at early in the film, when Jake meets Neytiri. He is clearly fascinated by her. But the key is when her mother recognizes something trustworthy in him. The fact that this high-priestess who is charged with protecting her people believes in him means that we believe in him. So when Jake accepts the assignment to be a spy, we know we are headed for something explosive. The build-up to that explosion powers Act Two; the explosion itself is Act Three.

In *Billy Elliot*, written by Lee Hall and directed by Stephen Daldry, Billy yearns to be a ballet dancer but lives in a working-class town where people are struggling to just get by. The visual manifestation of Billy's yearning comes right at the beginning of the film when he dances to his brother's record. Then he races out of the house to find his senile grandmother who has wandered off, and riot police fill the background of the shots. Billy's own widower father is being crushed by poverty during a strike at the local coal mine. By some measures, ballet seems beyond frivolous. The film is all about the contradiction between Billy and his circumstances. He is a gentle soul in a violent world. He learns about the ballet class in the gym where he is supposed to be learning to box. Billy learns to pirouette while his father and brother try to find a way to survive the endless miners' strike and the lines of riot police. Billy's father is nearly crushed by the burden of trying to feed his family and only decides to back his son's dreams after the heartbreaking scene when he realizes there is no hope for his own way of life. Billy is a perfect example of a character placed into circumstances in which he is least likely to succeed.

Note that in this film the writer put as much love and care into the creation of the antagonist as with the protagonist. Billy's father does everything he can to prohibit him from pursuing his dream. But he too has a humanizing contradiction. Billy's father, widowed and castrated by his inability to feed his family, has been boiled into a state of rigid rage and a worldview that does not extend beyond the borders of his tiny coal mining town, BUT he loves his family more than anything. At the end of the day it is Billy's optimism and passion that redeems both of them. The dynamic between the two characters is gripping, and the final moment when his father makes the trek to London to see his now-grown son make his first solo leap as the swan in *Swan Lake* is so emotional it induces goose bumps.

Amadeus was adapted by Peter Shaffer from his own stage play, and directed by Milos Forman. In it, a youthful and ambitious Antonio Salieri makes a pact with God, offering to trade absolute loyalty for musical genius. Believing that God has honored the pact, Salieri becomes court composer. He is humorless, ambitious, and pious — BUT he is also self-aware enough to understand instantly upon encountering Mozart that his talent is totally eclipsed by the younger man. God has betrayed him. He can't compose worth a damn, but is cursed with perfect appreciation of that which he can't achieve.

Mozart's contradictions are equally pronounced. He has prodigious gifts, but they are built upon the most fragile and damaged ego, which manifests as a vulgar, self-indulgent, and irreverent man-child. The contradictions in each character are like faults in a diamond that only needs the right tap to shatter. They get far more than a tap, because these characters are so completely opposite that their first meeting is like a collision of matter and anti-matter in which neither can really survive. The thrill of the film is watching them each disintegrate from cosmic forces far beyond their control, forces largely defined by these few broad strokes.

The main plot of the film is almost entirely carried on the backs of these contradictions. The day the young Salieri meets Mozart starts out with Salieri curious but confident in his role as court composer. Surely, God has granted him his boyhood wish of musical genius. The first time he sets eyes on Mozart he has no idea who he is, and is appalled by his vulgarity and immaturity. But then he hears his music and is instantly blown away by a sound he absolutely knows he can never achieve.

Salieri at first assumes this is a fluke — a strutting, uncouth twit like Mozart could not have such beauty locked inside him. But then he writes a march in Mozart's honor and Mozart, having memorized the piece in one casual hearing, proceeds to improvise a much more profound version of it.

The next blow comes when Salieri is given a chance to look through a pile of Mozart's original manuscripts and realizes that not only is the music beautiful enough to seem like "the voice of God," but there is not a single correction, "Like he was taking dictation." Salieri's sense of betrayal by the God he loved is solidified at that moment. Catalyzed by the revelation that Mozart has by now slept with the woman Salieri has lusted after but avoided because of his vow of chastity, he is galvanized into his plan to destroy the *enfant terrible*.

Do audiences need to love protagonists?

I want to pause a moment to talk about the difference between characters an audience likes and characters with whom audiences identify. Contrary to some of the literature, it is not necessary to give your protagonist a warm-and-fuzzy moment designed to make audiences like him/her — though to be fair it is harder to pull off a film with an unlikeable protagonist than with a likeable one. What you need to do is to make your audience identify with your protagonist, to connect with his/her humanity, even if he or she is a monster.

The greatest example I can think of is Martin Scorsese's *Raging Bull*, written by Paul Schrader and Mardik Martin based on the book by boxer Jake LaMotta and his collaborators. Robert De Niro played LaMotta, a man whose emotions were completely out of control. LaMotta was a great boxer, but violent bouts of jealousy destroyed his career and most of the important relationships in his life. And yet this film with a central character many people found repugnant is considered to be a modern classic.

Part of what made it work was the film's bookends. It opened with an older Jake LaMotta preparing to go on stage to do a comedy act and ends with this quote from the Bible:

> So, for the second time, [the Pharisees] summoned the man who had been blind and said:
> "Speak the truth before God. We know this fellow is a sinner."
> "Whether or not he is a sinner, I do not know," the man replied.
> "All I know is this: once I was blind and now I can see."
> — *The New English Bible*, John IX. 24–26

There is nothing funny about Jake in most of the film, and so part of what draws us in is curiosity — How did this beast wind up entertaining people? How did he come to a second chance as a comedian? We spend the movie waiting for his eyes to finally open so that he can stop destroying his own life and the lives of everyone who tries to love him. But also, all of us spend a certain amount of energy calming our rage, frustration, and fears. We identify with Jake because most of us work to hide the part of us that is him, and it is fascinating to watch a character so totally at the mercy of his emotions, so completely out of control. The man is a monster, not so cut off from his animal roots as the rest of us, but also utterly human, and we are drawn in watching him find some version of redemption.

Giving your protagonist certain quirks can also be an effective way to humanize your protagonist. I've already discussed the ice sculptures in *Edward Scissorhands*. Another example is in *Amadeus*. Protagonist Salieri is pompous, self-indulgent, cruel, and consumed by jealousy and narcissism. Not exactly a winning combination. Writer Peter Shaffer uses Salieri's love of sweets to humanize him. In the film's opening the servants describe the cakes they carry and moan in false ecstasy at their taste as a means to lure him to open his door. All of this lets us know that he is a petulant man-child. Then, when Old Salieri begins the tale of the events that led up to his suicide attempt, our first view of his younger self shows him swiping a sweet from a banquet table. It is a wonderfully funny beat for a character who is in other respects not so likeable. It is probably also the cue that made the actor (F. Murray Abraham) play Old Salieri as such a petulant, naughty child, smiling with such sadistic glee at the prospect of destroying the priest's faith through the re-telling of his story.

Tools of characterization

In creating your characters you have a number of tools at your disposal. There is some, but not total, overlap with the tools used by fiction writers. Screenwriters have to rely on what can be seen and heard since, with rare exception, they can give audiences no access to their characters' inner lives. There are exceptions to this rule. Screenwriter Akiva Goldsman found a brilliant way to give us access to schizophrenic mathematician John Nash's inner life in *A Beautiful Mind*. Woody Allen gave us a great look at what he was thinking in the dinner scene in *Annie Hall* when he showed us how his character imagined the others at the table saw him. In *Out of Africa*, screenwriter Kurt Luedtke used the occasional voice over to deepen our sense of protagonist Karen's thoughts. And author Michael Herr wrote genius narration for *Apocalypse Now* to both set the mood and tell us what was going on inside the head of Martin Sheen's Captain Willard. But these devices — hallucinations, voice over, and narration — need to be used only rarely and with caution since used incorrectly they can kill a film. As but one example, in the otherwise wonderful movie *Lord of War* by Andrew Niccol, the audience wound up distanced from the film because the emotional core of the story was relentlessly interrupted by the voice over.

In general, screenwriters need to rely upon what the audience can see or hear. The tools for characterization are, according to Janet Burroway and Elizabeth Stuckey-French in *Writing Fiction — A Guide to Narrative Craft*, appearance, action, dialogue, interpretation by another character, thought and authorial presentation. I have already discussed the difficulties of trying to indicate what a character is thinking.

So, let's discuss each of the other tools in some detail:

APPEARANCE: Appearance is what gives us our first impression of people. Everything they wear or own, how they hold themselves, how they move, how they use their faces and hands — all that presents some aspect of their inner selves. Appearance can present truth or it can embody the tension between appearance and reality. It is a hugely powerful tool for a writer. Burroway and Stuckey-French tell us,

> Concerned to see beyond mere appearances, writers are sometimes inclined to neglect this power of the visible. In fact, much of the tension and conflict in character does proceed from the truth that appearance is not reality. Features, shape, style, clothing and objects can make statements of internal values that are political, religious, social, intellectual, and essential. The man in the Ultra suede jacket is making a different statement from the one in the holey sweatshirt... The woman with the cigarette holder is telling us something different from the one with the palmed joint. Even a person who has forsaken our materialistic society altogether, sworn off supermarkets, and gone to the country to grow organic potatoes has a special relationship with his or her hoe. (page 82)

Screenwriters are, as in so much else, limited to how much space can be given over to character description. Details are vital, but lush paragraphs of them are death. So choosing exactly the right bits to reveal, the bits that are iconic for that character, is crucial. The goal is to draw the reader in, to give him/her enough food for the imagination so that the characters can spring to life in the readers' imaginations without so overwhelming them with detail that they are unable to draw their own conclusions or the read loses all energy and momentum... The questions is, what are the key characteristics you want to get across, and what few details will accomplish that?

Appearance includes sound and motion as well as sight. What does a name tell the reader about a character? How about how they move?

(Movement is different from action in that it does not advance the plot.) Describing a character's way of moving as feral or angry or aggressive helps fill in the picture.

In presenting a character's appearance, writers need to answer these questions:

- WHAT IS THEIR NAME? Not as easy as it seems. A name says a lot about a person. Is your protagonist exotic? Ethnic? A caricature? You can say so much with a name.

- WHAT IS THEIR GENDER? Also not always as easy as it seems. Would *Alien* have been as good if Ripley had been a guy? I promise you, someone at the studio raised the issue of whether or not you could make a successful action/suspense film with a "chick at the center."

- WHAT IS THEIR AGE? Lots more to weigh here than meets the eye. Remember who your first audience is. So you have to consider various factors: What is the appropriate age for the character you have in mind? The bigger the budget, the more you either have to consider how many "stars" there are in the age range you are writing for or make sure to write other roles that can be "stunt cast" with "names." Are the stars in the age bracket you are considering appealing to your target audience? Is the concept big enough to outweigh casting with low star power? Also, age can limit content. Terrible violence around children can be very difficult to pull off.

- WHAT DO THEY LOOK LIKE? How do they dress? Are they tall or short? Attractive or repulsive or somewhere in between? Are their strengths and weaknesses betrayed by their looks or do they come as a surprise? Do their looks help them or hinder them on their quest to get what they want?

ACTION: Action was the original basis of cinema, back before the age of "talkies." Charlie Chaplin's walk was to the character of The

Tramp what "Bond, James Bond" is to the James Bond character. It has been said, even now, that in a great film dialogue should act as subtitle, helping to sharpen what should already be clear through the action of the film. (I actually think the line would be better substituting "underscore" for "subtitles.")

Character-defining actions include:

- How does he/she move? Discussed above.

- How does he/she interact with people? Are they open or closed? Cranky of upbeat? Hospitable or curmudgeonly? Honest or guarded?

- What are their defining quirks? Does he or she have hobbies, tics, pet peeves, allergies...? How are they related to character?

- What are their predictable reactions to any given situation? In other words, how are their decisions defined by the character contradictions that define them?

- What are their actions that seem unpredictable, and what does that tell us about their state of mind?

I have written earlier about *The Fugitive* as a great example of the uses of action to define character and character to drive action. Dr. Richard Kimble is defined by his decision to risk his life on the doomed bus to save his jailor, by his decision to risk his freedom by stopping to help a sick kid in a hospital filled with cops searching for him, by his decision to make a probably fatal leap from the dam rather than call a halt to his pursuit of his wife's murderer. (Note: the repetition of the word "decision" is intentional and a not-so subtle hint.) And who he is determines the change in his antagonist's attitude and ultimately the course of the climatic action scene when U.S. Marshal Gerard breaks precedent and comes to Kimble's aid.

Burroway and Stuckey-French tell us, "The significant characters of a fiction must be both capable of causing an action and capable of being changed by it." This cause and effect — what a character does and how he/she reacts to the outcome of that action — is really what drives a story.

> If we accept that a story records a process of change, how is this change brought about? Basically, human beings face chance and choice, or discovery and decision — the first involuntary and the second voluntary. Translated into action, this means that a character driven by desire takes an action with an expected result, but something intervenes. Some force outside the character presents itself, in the form of information or accident or the behavior of others or the elements. The unknown becomes known, and then the discoverer must either take action or deliberately not take action, involving readers in the tension of the narrative query: and then what happens? (page 84)

Notice how this ties in to what I said was the advice of Matt Stone and Trey Parker: In a story, consecutive scenes must be linked either by "BUT THEN..." or "THEREFORE...." A character makes a discovery and THEREFORE takes an action (demanded by who he/she is), BUT THEN instead of the expected result something really bad happened, so he/she tries something else that results in a better outcome, THEREFORE he/she is able to take the next step in his/her journey, BUT THEN that next step is rendered pointless by the huge storm that falls... Character is action; action is character.

How much action detail are you required to describe? Again, balance is necessary. Every detail that comes to mind should not be in your script. Either you are the writer/director and you don't need to put in every last detail and motion because it is all in your head, or you are not and an overabundance will annoy the director who will want to take the distilled essence of your vision and transform it into his/her own. In either case, too much detail of setting or motion will deaden the read.

If detail is everything, but too much detail is death, how does one strike this balance? For me, the answer is to choose to describe only the defining details that will naturally flow into everything else the character does. For example, look at the following bit: He crosses the room slowly to the kitchen cabinet. He opens it. Chooses one of the mismatched coffee mugs. Puts it back, then chooses another. He examines it carefully. Carries it to the sink and washes some invisible spec from the lip before placing his one-cup coffee filter on top...

We know a lot about this guy from this description — the detailed accounting of his eccentric moves tells us he's a collector, a clean freak, a perfectionist. But you could only get away with one or two paragraphs like this before your reader would want to bludgeon you. So your decision as the writer should be, is what this tells us vital to understanding the character?

DIALOGUE: The first thing to say about dialogue in film is that there is a hidden trap embedded in the process of creating it. Even though visual language takes primacy in film, dialogue can have an outsized impact both positive and negative. What, for example, would Aaron Sorkin's *A Few Good Men* be without Jack Nicholson's "You can't handle the truth" speech? The pitfall is new writers' tendency to use dialogue purely as a means of delivering information.

How a person speaks can tell us place and era of origin, level of education, level of compassion and pomposity and humor and commitment, shyness, warmth. But also, dialogue has in common with appearance the potential to contradict reality. Even more than with appearance, much of the tension in a story comes from the distance that can exist between what a character says and what he/she actually does. A huge part of the fun of Rossio and Elliott's *Pirates of the Caribbean* comes from the thought that is repeatedly raised about Johnny Depp's Captain Jack Sparrow, "He's lying... or is he?" In Robert Towne's *Chinatown*, Evelyn Mulwray (played by Faye Dunaway) is dangerous because she is both seductive and deranged — nothing she says turns out to be true.

Dialogue in film often carries a different burden than it does in fiction. Fiction writers are free to use narration to deliver exposition, a gift rarely given to screenwriters. In screenplays, exposition must be embedded either in a dramatic scene or in the visuals. But a character ceases to be a real character if all he/she does is explain stuff. In *The Fugitive*, Tommy Lee Jones' Marshal Gerard delivers an entire paragraph of exposition about what is going to be done to capture Richard Kimble...

> MARSHAL GERARD
> Ladies and gentlemen... our fugitive's been on the run for ninety minutes. Average foot speed over uneven ground — barring injury is approximately four miles an hour, giving us a radius of six miles. I want a hard-target search of any residence, gas station, farmhouse, henhouse, doghouse and outhouse in that area. Check-points go up at 15 miles. Go get him.

...but it doesn't read like exposition because it is planted inside a dramatic scene..

Burroway and Stuckey-French tell us...

> Because direct dialogue has a dual nature — emotion within a logical structure — its purpose in fiction is never merely to convey information. Dialogue may do that... but it needs simultaneously to characterize, provide exposition, set the scene, advance the action, foreshadow, and/or remind... Dialogue, therefore, is not just transcribed speech, it is *distilled* speech — the 'filler' and inert small talk of real conversation is edited away, even as the weight of the implication is increased." (page 88)

Some of the best dialogue is powerful precisely because it avoids the truth. "Dialogue can fall flat if characters define their feelings too precisely and honestly, because often the purpose of human exchange is to conceal as well as to reveal — to impress, hurt, protect, seduce, or reject. Anton Chekhov believed that a line of dialogue should always leave the sense that more could have been said. Playwright David

Mamet suggests that someone may or may not say what they mean, but "always says something designed to get what they want." (page 92)

An important point to remember about dialogue is that it is designed to heighten the drama of a scene, to heighten the conflict. Part of the art of writing is in knowing how to dole out information.

> When an unspoken subject remains unspoken, tension continues to build in a story. Often the crisis of a story occurs when the unspoken tension comes to the surface and an explosion results. "If you're trying to build pressure, don't take the lid off the pot," Jerome Stern suggests in his book *Making Shapely Fiction*. "Once people are really candid, once the unstated becomes stated, the tension is released and the effect is cathartic... you want to give yourself the space for a major scene. Here you do want to describe setting and action vividly, and render what they say fully. You've taken the lid off the pot and we want to feel the dialogue boil over." (page 93)

In dialogue, specificity is as important as it is in description. We tend to believe concrete details, which can also be the stuff of great conflict, especially as characters dig up old memories. Look, for example, at some of Old Salieri's speeches in *Amadeus*. Here, he is bemoaning the fact that Vogler, the priest who has come to hear his confession after he attempted suicide, can't recall a single melody Salieri wrote.

OLD SALIERI
Can you recall no melody of mine? I was
the most famous composer in Europe when
you were still a boy. I wrote forty operas
alone. What about this little thing?

Writer Peter Shaffer has managed to embed exposition in dramatic context. And the speech is given real weight by the single detail that he wrote "forty operas alone." His claim that he was the most famous composer in Europe might have felt like empty boasting but for that one detail.

Here he is again describing Mozart, the genius he is about to meet.

```
             OLD SALIERI
As I went through the salon, I played a
game with myself. This man had written his
first concerto at the age of four; his first
symphony at seven; a full-scale opera at
twelve. Did it show? Is talent like that
written on the face?
```

This speech accomplishes so much. It gives us the details of Mozart's prodigy in a way that does not seem like exposition because those details are part of a dramatic story, steps leading up to Salieri's first encounter with his hero. Those same details help set up our expectations of Mozart far more than if Salieri had simply described the man as a genius — the details make us believe his claim. And then the speech ends by posing one of the primary thematic questions of the film, "Is talent like that written on the face?"

INTERPRETATION BY ANOTHER CHARACTER: A character may also be introduced or characterized through the opinions of other characters. There is not too much to say about this. Both the character being described and the one doing the describing can come alive through this method — how someone reacts to someone else can tell us a lot about them. And of course the extent to which we believe a character's description depends upon how we feel about the one doing the describing.

Interpretation by another character is one of the means you have for delivering backstory. "He was married, you know," tells us a bit of a character's history. And you can add a whole other layer by describing the tone in which the information is delivered — Catty? Sympathetic? As mentioned earlier, this is precisely how the secret in *The Fugitive* was delivered, in an eyebrow-raising conversation between Kimble's "friend" Dr. Nichols and Nichols' business partner, Dr. Lentz.

AUTHORIAL PRESENTATION: Authorial presentation is far more available to writers of other genres than to dramatic writers. A sentence of description like, "She feels far more than she shows," is a cue to an actress about the character she is playing. It is something we can see in a performance and so can work in a script. But lines like, "She knows he's lying," which you could easily write in a novel, is much less relevant in a screenplay. Lines like that raise the question in the reader, "How will we know that?" So authorial presentation needs to be used judiciously or it starts to seem like the work of a lazy writer who hasn't figured out how to dramatize the emotions of his/her story.

The relationship between structure and character

There is a powerful relationship between structure and character:

• The inciting incident needs to determine what your protagonist wants at the end of Act One. This MUST be defined as succinctly and clearly as possible. The "want" defines the trajectory at the start of Act Two. If you don't know the answer, don't write the script.

Some writers get tripped up by defining the want either too narrowly or too imprecisely. You can't switch wants once you set one, you can only switch approaches. A character might think he or she wants one thing at the end of Act One and then discover they really need something else, but both must be paths to the same goal. For example, a character who avoids all emotional attachment for three quarters of a film, only to discover at the end of Act Two that he is in love with the woman he has been pushing away for all of Act Two, is probably really a character so in need of love that when we meet him he's too terrified of getting hurt to risk attachment. So we might say that what he wanted at the start of the film was a life that was safe from hurt but realized in the end that life without love hurts more than anything.

You want to be extremely precise in defining your character's want. For example, in *The Fugitive*, after Richard Kimble's wife is murdered, he's falsely accused and convicted. It would be easy to assume that what he wants is vengeance. But that's not Kimble. He wants justice. That difference is a big part of what defines his character, as we'll see later in the book.

• The beat of hesitation that occurs before the protagonist decides to take the opportunity offered by the first plot point is often where we discover what the character needs (as opposed to wants). There are other ways to describe "need." What is the character flaw that threatens to prevent your protagonist from getting what he or she wants? What is it that she really needs that she is too wounded or too scared or too selfish to admit?

The dialectic between the need and the want is often a big part of the key to building tension in your story. It sets the audience up to worry that the character to whom they have bonded will repeatedly do stupid stuff that is decidedly not in their best interest. The fact that an audience will recognize this kind of behavior in themselves only helps people bond to your characters. If you've done your job, you can have the audience silently screaming at your protagonist, "Don't do that again!" And sigh with relief when the protagonist finally gets it.

Other important character issues for Act One

WHAT IS YOUR PROTAGONIST'S BACKSTORY?

This is something you need to know in order to create a rich, fully fleshed-out character. It is a different matter entirely to decide how much of that history needs to be revealed in the film. Sometimes the entirety of the backstory that will be in the film is presented in Act One. In other films, it is doled out throughout the film, each piece presented at the last minute as it is needed to push the plot forward.

In *The Fugitive*, we don't care at all about what made Kimble or Gerard into the people they are. There is simply no time to establish their histories since in that film momentum is everything. So everything we know about Kimble is presented in Act One.

Amadeus is the opposite. We learn through flashbacks and narration about the pact Salieri made when he asked God to grant him musical genius great enough to make his name immortal. This is crucial to understanding Salieri as the embodiment of the film's theme that God is impervious to man's wants. Similarly, the flashbacks that illuminated Mozart's difficult relationship with his ambitious and intolerant father help us relate to and feel compassion for a character who is at base something of an ass.

A rule to remember regarding backstory: Only reveal those parts of a character's history that are crucial to your story or that would diminish an audience's ability to understand the piece by their absence.

The strongest tools for presenting backstory are presenting it through dramatic (as opposed to purely expositional) dialogue or interpretation by other characters. The impact of a character's history, of course, is also embedded in how they act. Narration, voice over, and flashbacks are also available methods but should be used with caution as they can seem lazy.

WHAT IS THE PROTAGONIST'S
KEY EMOTIONAL RELATIONSHIP?

Pretty much every film has one, even the ones that don't look like they do. Sometimes it is a standard love story — but not always. There is no running romance *per se* in *The Fugitive* but there is a powerful story of the growing respect Gerard feels as he tries to understand the motives of a fugitive who proves to be clearly good. In *The King's Speech* it is the budding friendship between the future King of England and his speech therapist. Since you can't introduce either a main character or subplot late in the film, **this relationship needs to be set up either in Act One or very early in Act Two.**

WHO IS YOUR ANTAGONIST, WHAT DO
THEY WANT, WHAT DO THEY NEED?

Your protagonist is partly defined by their antagonist, by the forces he or she needs to overcome in order to get what they want. The main thing to keep in mind about your antagonist is this: Protagonist and antagonist must be worthy adversaries. Your antagonist must be so good at getting in your protagonist's way that your protagonist's success is really in doubt. The better the antagonist, the higher your protagonist will have to rise to meet the challenge and so the better the film. **The antagonist is always introduced in Act One or early in Act Two, right after the protagonist decides to take the opportunity offered by the first plot point.**

Note that antagonists who are just bad for the sake of being bad rarely work outside of James Bond films. They must have an agenda and a flaw that is as specific as your protagonist's. All of the questions I am asking about the protagonist should be asked in reference to the antagonist as well. But in addition, what is it about the antagonist that humanizes them? What is their good quality? In what way does their character speak to your premise?

Note, too, that many fledgling screenwriters insist that their protagonist's flaw makes them their own worst enemy and therefore the antagonist of the film. This is almost never the case. (It might have been true in *Raging Bull*.) Your protagonist almost always needs to have some flaw that they will trip over through most of the film. (Even perfect Superman has his Kryptonite.) But this does not in any way excuse the writer from the task of creating a separate antagonist who can INTENTIONALLY get in your protagonist's way.

Entrances

There are obviously a lot of factors involved in creating castable characters. A compelling journey, intriguing character contradictions, a great romance, great lines — all of these improve both your script and your chances of locking in talent. In addition, there is nothing wrong with giving your lead a terrific entrance. An example of the most obvious version of what I'm talking about: In *Troy*, writer David Benioff opened his film with a scene of a marauding giant that no one could defeat. "Get Achilles," someone said, and off some servant boy ran to roust our protagonist. Achilles rose from his bed, leaving two naked beauties behind, strode out to the battlefield with total confidence, leapt onto the giant's shoulders, and killed the beast before anyone knew what had happened. The script had barely begun, but it is my guess that Brad Pitt was "in" by the end of that sequence.

It is decidedly not necessary to be this obvious or this crass. My point is, part of your job as screenwriter is to hook actor talent and this is not a simple task. Great entrances, powerful and unique characters in extreme situations and plagued by compelling contradictions, great voices — these are all things you should keep in mind when creating your characters.

Secondary characters

One of the components that makes *The Fugitive* work so well is Marshal Gerard's posse, a cast of characters that director Andy Davis had to fight the studio to keep. Gerard's sidekicks are each distinct. There is something loopy about how they relate and something threatening about their efficiency and dedication to their jobs. Andy cast them perfectly — but the things I want you to notice are the richness of the portraits and the efficiency with which they are set up. They are types — the rookie, the serious cop, the irreverent one who can joke with the boss — but they are not cardboard cutouts. Each has a personality. We like them because they want to do their jobs well. Despite the fact that Gerard is the antagonist, he is human and we rather like the guy, and so we like the group that is trying to help him. The moment when the rookie is taken hostage and Gerard shoots the criminal holding him works so well because we've come to love the rookie's innocence and sincerity. Playing off his frightened face when Gerard says, "I... don't... negotiate..." makes Gerard's statement of rigidity all the more terrifying — we know that Kimble is in deep trouble if this guy catches up to him. It wouldn't work as well if the posse wasn't so wonderfully drawn. At the same time, note that we don't spend a second with that group if it doesn't directly move the story forward.

Secondary characters and subplots are constructed with the same toolbox used to build the protagonist and antagonist. They run the gamut, from the guys we know nothing about in *Star Trek* and who are only cast so they can be killed, to the secondary characters in a film like *Amadeus* who are pretty fully fleshed out and who carry complete subplots that wrap around and support the main plot.

One of the traps that I see writers fall into with some regularity is that they confuse the notions of complex and complicated. Complicated is defined as a script that has too much going on that doesn't have much to do with the main story — extra characters, extra subplots that seem fun or interesting but that don't really advance the main story. Complex scripts, on the other hand, are packed with subtleties and well-developed secondary characters with interesting storylines that actually enrich the main plot.

The first question to ask yourself with regard to how you have used secondary characters and subplots is, would your main story play any less well if the film editor left every frame related to a secondary storyline on the cutting room floor? If the answer is yes, then the subplot and characters have to go.

There is an exception to this rule. In a comedy you can do stuff for the sole reason of getting a laugh. The animated film *Ice Age* is a great example. There is a whole running gag about a character called Scrat. Scrat has absolutely nothing to do with the main plot. But the bits in which he pops up are hysterical. Not only do they belong in the film — Scrat has come to define the entire franchise.

But that is the exception. In general, subplots need to impact your main storyline in organic and important ways. A film like *Amadeus*, for example, is a much more complex story than *The Fugitive*, which basically has one story to follow and rarely leaves the POV of either Kimble or Gerard. *Amadeus* skips between time periods and runs a plethora of interlocking and parallel subplots with a myriad of characters. And yet it has the same clarity and sharpness of focus as *The Fugitive*. Each subplot is crystal clear because each character is painted with such precision, and because the various subplots and characters are so beautifully intertwined to build on one another.

EXERCISES

Creating your character bible

The following exercises are written about your protagonist, but they should be done for every major character in your film. Secondary characters don't need as much detail. What you want to wind up with is a living character bible that gets updated as the writing progresses. This character bible is not part of the outline, but it helps determine its shape because characters should behave in your script according to the strengths and weaknesses laid out in the bible.

1. What are the basics of your protagonist's identity?
   a. What is the protagonist's name?
   b. What is their gender.
   c. What is their age?
   d. Describe what he/she looks like. Does their look mask or highlight their character?
   e. What are your protagonist's defining quirks?
   f. How does your protagonist interact with people?
   g. What is their level of education? Where do they come from? How is that embedded in how they speak and dress and move?

2. Write about your protagonist's defining contradiction. In what way is your protagonist unequipped or overmatched for the journey ahead? This is what professor and screenwriter Neil Landau calls "the hook" of the film, the bit that will become the part of your pitch most likely to get your audience invested.

3. Write about what your protagonist wants versus what he/she needs. What are his/her flaws that will stand in the way of getting what he/she wants? This is not necessarily the same as the contradiction. Billy Elliot's defining contradiction is that he was born with an artist's soul but lives in an impoverished and macho working-class town. His *want* is to become a ballet

dancer — but first he *needs* to learn that it is possible for his dreams to come true if he lives according to his heart.

4. What defines your protagonist's life before the inciting incident? What is his/her like when we meet him or her? What is most important to him/her?

5. Write about your protagonist's backstory. Start thinking about which parts of that will be necessary to tell or show the reader.

6. Write a sales pitch to an actor. Why should he or she consider the role in your film over all the others being offered?

7. Do all the same exercises regarding the antagonist and the object of the key emotional relationship.

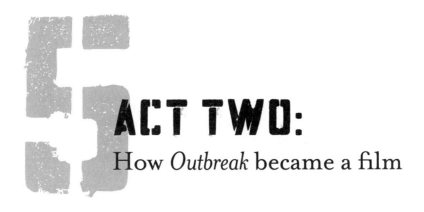

ACT TWO:
How *Outbreak* became a film

A film's Act Two contains most of the protagonist's journey toward what he/she wants. As discussed earlier, it is divided roughly into two movements, with the first half (Act 2a) seeming to go relatively well for the protagonist and the second half (Act 2b) driving the protagonist nearly to despair.

Here is a more detailed shape of Act Two:

- ACKNOWLEDGING THE RISK: Your protagonist comes out of Act One having made the decision to take the first plot point's potentially life-changing or life-threatening opportunity to reach their goal. This comes after your protagonist has taken a beat to consider that decision. The hesitation is your protagonist acknowledging that he/she knows the journey ahead will not be easy and cues the audience that he/she will be heading out of their comfort zone.

- THE "ROAD RUNNER": Remember those "Road Runner" cartoons from Looney Tunes? The Road Runner would race down the road, Wile E. Coyote would set up some Acme creation to trap or thwart the Road Runner — and fail every time. This is sort of what happens in Act 2a of your script, with a few major differences. Your "Road Runner," or protagonist, will have a very specific goal at each step. And whereas each challenge in the cartoon was just another gag, in your screenplay the level of difficulty at each step will escalate.

- Act 2a officially begins when your protagonist takes his/her first step toward their goal. By doing what? By doing the most obvious thing he/she can do to move forward. But then...

- THE ANTAGONIST (if he/she has not been introduced in Act Two, this needs to happen in the beginning of Act 2a) takes his or her first step toward thwarting your protagonist. BUT your protagonist's first step will be relatively successful, leaving the antagonist thwarted instead.

  - This game of leapfrog between protagonist and antagonist forms a series of **sequences**. There are usually four to six of these reverses in Act 2a. Your protagonist will get increasingly confident and your antagonist will become increasingly frustrated. Not that this period will be without pitfalls for your protagonist. The antagonist needs to be formidable throughout. But both reader and protagonist will think all is going pretty well until...

- THE MIDPOINT: At the midpoint of both the script and Act Two, something happens that spins your protagonist in a new direction and gives your antagonist a new window of opportunity. Although the literature cleverly calls this the "midpoint," it essentially acts like another plot point. The midpoint can be something your protagonist does, a revelation, or something that happens to change the landscape. This changed dynamic implies increased danger and heightened stakes. The midpoint launches...

- ACT 2B: Your protagonist will emerge from the midpoint with a more focused plan for reaching his or her goal, while your antagonist will have a clearer shot at success. So in Act 2b (the script's third quarter) things will become increasingly dangerous for your protagonist. Progress will be both steadier and more fraught. Things will become more dangerous, whatever that means in the context of the kind of film you are writing. Your protagonist will need to rise to ever more intense levels to stay ahead of the antagonist and keep moving forward, as if the air he or she moves through has suddenly gotten denser and more resistant to movement, until...

- THE LOW POINT: At the end of Act Two it will look like your protagonist's defeat is inevitable. Knowing what your protagonist wants and needs and the secret that needs to be revealed, what is the absolute worst thing that your protagonist can either realize or encounter on the road to achieving their goal? This "all is lost" moment acts like another inciting incident, creating the circumstances for...

- THE SECOND PLOT POINT: This is the moment when your protagonist realizes that there is one final, all-or-nothing opportunity to achieve his or her objective. Again, there is usually a beat of hesitation, more profound than at the first plot point, acknowledging that the opportunity being afforded is the end of the line, that the stakes could not be higher. The second plot point marks the end of Act Two. The decision to take that final chance launches Act Three.

Act Two is where a lot of writers lose steam. Some people blame this on the fact that there appear to be fewer guideposts to mark the path than in Act One. You have to create twenty-five to thirty pages of things seeming to go well for your protagonist, and twenty-five to thirty more where things get increasingly difficult, with only the midpoint, low point, and second plot point to guide you. It seems hard to sustain. But it doesn't need to be. I believe that if you do your work well in Act One, then there will be more to go on in Act Two than might be apparent upon first glance.

Other components of Act Two

THE KEY EMOTIONAL RELATIONSHIP: If this was not introduced in Act One then it must be begin near the top of Act Two.

THE COMING TOGETHER OF WANT AND NEED: At some point in Act Two the protagonist will need to come face to face with his or her main character flaw, the thing that is stopping him/her from seeing or accomplishing the obvious. This usually happens toward the end of Act Two. These moments of illumination can be enormously energizing and should be saved for use when they are most needed or most effective.

TICKING CLOCK: One of my favorite stories from the trenches was told to me by the Oscar-winning screenwriter Brian Helgeland (*L.A. Confidential*). Early in his career he was hired to work on a film already in production in Italy. Brian was there to make sense of what had been shot and integrate it into new scenes. The thing that kept stumping him was that in a car that was important to the story there was always a wind-up alarm clock on the dashboard. Brian finally asked the director what that was about. And the director replied something on the order of, "I was told that you Americans always have a ticking clock in your movies."

The misunderstanding is hilarious because it is based in a kernel of truth: Most American films set up a deadline before which the protagonist must accomplish his or her goal. Get the girl before she leaves town or marries someone else; kill the bad guy before he kills you; find the real killer before you're arrested for the murder others think you committed. This clock is usually wound early in Act Two, right around the point that your protagonist accepts the challenge of the first plot point.

REVELATION OF THE SECRET AT THE HEART OF YOUR FILM: As discussed earlier, most films have a secret that comes to light over the course of the movie, usually late in Act Two. Sometimes it is a pure mystery as in *Chinatown* in which the entire film is a search for the man who killed Hollis Mulwray. Sometimes it is a reveal that what you thought you were seeing is really something else entirely, such as in *The Sixth Sense* in which Bruce Willis' character turned out to be a ghost. Sometimes the audience is ahead of the characters and sometimes the reveal happens for audience and characters at the same moment.

The decision regarding when you flip the card on the reveal depends on whether you are aiming for suspense or surprise. If the audience learns a dangerous truth about an antagonist ahead of the protagonist then it will anticipate trouble and root for the protagonist to discover the truth in time. *Sixth Sense,* on the other hand, was not about suspense. The satisfaction of that movie came from being surprised and then replaying the film and having all of the slightly discordant beats make sense in light of the reveal.

Reveals can never appear to come from out of nowhere. The trick to making reveals work is to make sure you lay in clues that play one way the first time an audience sees them but that can be reinterpreted at the moment of the reveal when the audience does an instant replay of the film to see if it all adds up. Sometimes this relates to plot, as in *Iron Man,* when Tony Stark realizes his father's business partner is really his enemy. Or in *Little Miss Sunshine,* when Olive's family realizes that her grandfather trained her to do a far-too-adult dance for her beauty pageant. Other times it's a character beat in which your protagonist has a revelation about his or her own character that helps him or her rise to the challenge of the third act, as in *Butch Cassidy and the Sundance Kid* when Butch and Sundance realize that they are dinosaurs — that the world has passed them by and left no place in it for people like them. In either case, these are major turning points in the film.

The rhythm of Act Two

Producer Joel Silver (*The Matrix, Lethal Weapon*) famously insists that in an action film Act Two must be peppered with explosions every ten to fifteen pages. While this formula has become something of a cliché, it is also true that you need to regularly ignite the fuel that powers your story — and this does not just apply to action films. There are lots of ways to do this: revealing the film's secret, delivering a moment of self-revelation for the characters, creating a surprise twist in the plot or a moment that is stunningly visual or wildly funny or completely terrifying or deeply emotional. As you design your Act Two you need to drop these things in as needed.

What does "as needed" mean? I'm told that DreamWorks Animation king and former Disney studio chief Jeffrey Katzenberg puts the storyboards for his films up on the studio walls and then runs colored yarn above them in a graph that indicates emotional and energy highs and lows. Too long in any one state is deadly, just like music with no variation of rhythm or tempo or dynamics can be gruesome to hear. The trick is to use the kinds of beats mentioned above as mini-plot points that spin the mood in some new direction. If we're up we need to be down; if we're serious we need to be funny; if we're safe we need to be in danger. If we're frustrated then at some point we need a revelation to bring us relief.

Some of these energizing moments I'm talking about can also be — guess what — the all-important trailer moments. So in your writing, push yourself to deliver the most original version of these moments. As an example, in the diner scene in *When Harry Met Sally...*, Meg Ryan could simply have told Billy Crystal that women were perfectly capable of faking an orgasm. It would have worked — and no one would remember the scene. Having Meg fake an orgasm right there at the table, though... no one who has seen it forgets that scene.

Remember, you are not writing a script for a stage play; you are writing a script for the screen. Take advantage of the medium when you can. Give your actors the gift of great, original visual and visceral moments when you can. Push yourself always.

And always remember the rhythm discussed at length earlier. Each scene needs to compel the next with either a "BUT THEN..." or a "THEREFORE...."

Tips from the pits of development hell — creating an Act Two that doesn't unravel

Act Two trouble usually has one of two points of origin. Either Act One has not done its job, or the through line is not connected firmly enough to what was set up in Act One. So, some tips:

• Really hang on to what you set up in Act One. Let your protagonist be driven by what he/she wants and endangered by his/her flaws. Let him/her be torn by his/her contradiction, and by the difference between want and need.

- Keep it simple.

- Keep your theme firmly in mind. Each move your protagonist makes should be an expression of that theme.

- Be aware of the music of the act, the rhythm of reverses, the contrast between high energy and low energy scenes/sequences.

- Your goal is to continue to ratchet up the tension.

Analysis — Act Two of *The Fugitive*

One of the things to notice in the following analysis of *The Fugitive* is how much of Act Two was determined by Act One. As a reminder, from Act One we know...

- Kimble's only clues as to the identity of the killer are the memories he has of the one-armed man.

- The fact that Kimble is a doctor means he knows more than most about where in Chicago one would most likely visit to get and service a prosthetic arm.

So the writers would have known that in the broadest sense Kimble's goals would need to be to make his way to Chicago, find a list of likely suspects, and investigate those suspects until the secret set up in Act One is revealed — that the hit was really ordered by his "friend" Dr. Nichols. They could have dropped these beats into an outline...

- Kimble has to escape the site of the crash, with Federal Marshal Gerard's deft pursuit providing the ticking clock. Note that his goal is singular and made more difficult by his own character contradiction — he is a man on the run, with no experience as a fugitive, and yet he is compelled to help everyone who needs him...

- Act 2a will be all about Kimble making his way to the clinic where he can obtain a list of one-armed men, while staying ahead of Gerard.

- The midpoint will be when Kimble arrives in Chicago. Now he is no longer running from Gerard; he is moving toward his suspect. Gerard can start to figure out his motive and therefore try to get a step ahead of him.

- Act 2b will be Kimble getting his list and investigating the names on it.

- The low point will be Kimble's discovery that the one-armed man was hired by the drug company whose research project Kimble had been looking into.

- The second plot point will be the opportunity to follow up on this new lead. The decision to do so rather than reporting his discovery to the Feds is the beginning of the third act.

And all of these steps can be made more dangerous because Gerard is so good at his job, and because Kimble's character compels him to stop and do the right thing even when doing so isn't in his best interest. That's a lot of guideposts derived from Act One. Let's look how this information actually translates into sequences:

- Sequence 1 — Kimble on the run/Gerard sets up the pursuit: We know from the set-up that Kimble will be a virgin fugitive, which means that when he first flees he will be acting almost entirely from fear. Like a fox in a British hunt, all he'll be able to do is run and search for a place that instinctively spells safety — in Kimble's case, a hospital. On the other hand, we see as soon as we meet Gerard that he and his team are experienced and efficient. So the opening of Act Two is almost pre-ordained: Kimble will flee while Gerard barks orders that establish a search and a perimeter meant to box Kimble in. This is the first sequence of Act 2a, and like all these sequences it has its own beginning, middle, and end.

This is a high energy sequence. In the end, Kimble makes it to the perceived safety of a hospital. BUT THEN...

• Sequence 2 — The hospital is crawling with cops/Kimble gets a disguise/Gerard gets the word out: Even a virgin fugitive knows that the first thing he has to do is to get rid of his prison clothes. Note that this is a much lower energy sequence than the escape from the bus. Still, it's a pretty simple step — get a disguise — in which a lot happens:

  · Kimble makes it to the hospital, but the place is filled with cops. Kimble gets inside, BUT THEN the fax machine spits out his photo. The concern that he will be recognized is ratcheted up when he passes a cop carrying the fax of his photo, but he gets by safely. THEREFORE...

  · Kimble gets a change of clothes and the tools he needs to close up his wound. BUT THEN...

  · On the way out of the hospital he passes an ambulance where the guard whose life he saved is being unloaded. Kimble is nearly busted, but he slaps an oxygen mask over the guard's face. Therefore, Kimble is able to take the next step...

• Sequence 3 — Kimble starts his trek toward Chicago/Gerard pursues him: Disguised and having seemingly slipped past the law, Kimble needs to get back to Chicago. THEREFORE, he steals the ambulance that was carrying the guard. BUT THEN the theft is immediately reported to Gerard. The ensuing chase ends when it looks like Kimble is trapped. BUT THEN he makes his extraordinary leap from the dam. This is a high-energy sequence.

  · Note that this third sequence has considerably more tension than the first. Gerard very nearly nails Kimble. Things have escalated.

  · Note too that in the Kimble/Gerard bromance subplot, the inciting incident was Gerard's arrival at the crash site. Kimble's leap from the dam is the first plot point, upsetting Gerard's absolutist view of the world in which he operates. Kimble's leap makes no sense to Gerard, and he will spend the rest of the film trying to understand the guy.

- Sequence 4 — Kimble heads toward Chicago/Gerard loses the scent: Notice how the energy of these sequences continues to alternate. This is another low-energy one. Kimble survived the leap and escaped Gerard, so things are going pretty well for him. In fact, Gerard is the only person on his team who believes Kimble might still be alive. THEREFORE, Kimble has bought himself the space to pursue his search. He is no longer running from Gerard, he is racing to find the one-armed man, and at this moment Gerard has no way to follow him, no clue where he is headed. The steps of the sequence are:
  - Kimble dyes his hair.
  - Kimble accepts a ride into Chicago from a woman. (This was all that remained of the waitress character cut from the script.) Note that these two scenes break the Stone/Parker rule — they are linked by "and then." The sequence provides a brief breather. The point here is to get Kimble to Chicago. Kimble's journey is pretty uneventful at this point, so the sequence gets goosed when Gerard gets word the cops have "found the woman's car," a great misdirect that made the audience believe Kimble was in real danger. Instead, Gerard and his team head out — and surround a different fugitive, another of the escaped prisoners. The guy grabs one of Gerard's men and tries to negotiate. Gerard kills him, later telling his deputy, "I don't bargain." This is the entire point of the sequence: to raise the stakes for Kimble. At this moment, we know that Gerard will shoot Richard Kimble dead if he has the opportunity.

- Sequence 5 — MIDPOINT — Kimble gets settled in Chicago/ Gerard figures out he is back:
  - Kimble makes it to Chicago, but he has no money. Therefore, he phones his attorney to ask for help. BUT THEN the attorney, who was set up in Act One as an ineffectual ally, refuses to help

— and Gerard, who has tapped the attorney's phone, overhears the conversation. Gerard and his team figure out that Kimble has come home. Kimble is a step closer to his goal, but also a step closer to being in Gerard's sites. Note that this is a second step in Gerard's growing appreciation for the fact that Kimble is not behaving like a guilty man — if he killed his wife, why would he return to Chicago? Gerard is determined not to care, but he is at heart a fair man and so this inconsistency cannot help but bug him.

- Turned away by his lawyer, Kimble needs to try something else and so flags down Nichols in his car and asks for cash. Nichols acts surprised — but later we will realize he was in reality horrified — to learn Richard is still alive. This scene plays two roles, both determined by Act One. Kimble was a prisoner and so needs cash for food and shelter. But also, when the film's big secret that Nichols ordered the hit is revealed, the audience will replay the film to see if everything really adds up. Moments like Nichols' reaction that can be reinterpreted later help to make the reveal credible and satisfying, as opposed to contrived.

- Kimble now has some money and therefore rents a shitty apartment from a Polish woman and her disreputable son. At the same time, Gerard re-opens the murder investigation. Questions the Chicago cops. Questions Nichols, who admits to having seen Kimble but insists he is both innocent and too smart to get caught.

- Cook County Hospital: Kimble scopes out the Myoelectric Institute where prosthetics are built and fitted to patients. Only a doctor would know where to go or have enough understanding of how a hospital works to find a way in. Meanwhile, a room full of cops is told that Kimble is back...

- MONTAGE: Kimble prepares a disguise and does research that will inform his search while Gerard tightens the net. The montage ends when Kimble is awakened from a nightmare to find his apartment surrounded by cops. Kimble is terrified for a moment — but it turns out that the cops are actually after his landlady's drug-dealing son. THEREFORE...

- Kimble has his false identification and is able to get his list of one-armed suspects from Cook County Hospital. But back at the station the cops question the Polish drug dealer. He reveals that Kimble rented an apartment from his mother. Therefore, Gerard raids the apartment, discovers evidence of the Cook County Hospital badge Kimble made, and heads over there.
- Kimble has his information and should flee the hospital, but when he is leaving he finds the emergency room flooded with victims of some disaster. True to his character, he stops to save a young boy's life. He is nearly busted, but finally escapes with his list. Gerard shows up moments later, stunned again to learn that the guy stopped to help someone. He is unable to figure out what Kimble was doing there until he sees and follows a one-armed man. Not long after, Gerard also has the same list of suspects. Kimble's and Gerard's paths are converging. **This is the moment that flips the story in a new direction of the act — the true midpoint.**

- Sequence 6 — Start of Act 2b — Kimble and Gerard each run through their lists: One person on the list is dead. The next is incarcerated in the county jail, a building filled to bursting with cops. Kimble sucks it up and goes in. Gerard is not far behind. Even his guys are starting to figure out that Kimble's actions make no sense if he is guilty. Kimble is very nearly captured by Gerard. This close call is the first step in the things-stop-going-so-well part of Act 2b.

- Sequence 7 — Kimble finds the one-armed man/Gerard misses his man:
  - Kimble has one more name — Sykes. Gerard has Sykes' house staked out, but Kimble sneaks in the back, searches the place — and discovers a photo of Sykes on vacation with a guy named Lentz, the Devlin-MacGregor executive to whom Nichols

introduced him back in Act One. Kimble also finds evidence that Sykes is on the Devlin-MacGregor payroll. This is **the low point** — Kimble realizes he has been on the wrong trail.

· Kimble leaves a clue that will lure Gerard to the same discovery while he heads to the hospital to confirm his worst fears — his "best friend" Nichols is the bad guy. That discovery provides **the second plot point** when Kimble learns where Nichols is. Kimble's decision to confront the guy launches us into Act Three.

An interesting side-note: If Kimble had merely been after revenge, he would have hung around to kill Sykes. But he was after justice. So he phoned Gerard and left the phone off the hook so Gerard could trace the call. Kimble then headed off on this new path — he wanted to make certain he was right.

Another tale from the trenches: *Outbreak* — how a key Act Two decision won a war between studios

There are mixed opinions of *Outbreak*, written by Laurence Dworet and Robert Roy Pool and directed by Wolfgang Petersen. So for those of you familiar with the film, try to put aside whatever you do or do not think of as its failings for a moment. The story of its birth is both remarkable and instructional.

Here, as a starting point, is what Wikipedia has to say about the film:

> "Crisis in the Hot Zone" was the title of a 1992 non-fiction article by Richard Preston in *The New Yorker*. It chronicles the story of how the U.S. government believed a deadly virus had entered the United States.
>
> The article was later expanded into the 1994 book *The Hot Zone*. The article created a bidding war between rival movie studios for the film rights. The rights were sold to 20th Century Fox and producer Lynda Obst on the understanding

that as a woman she would be able to treat the lead character — a female government scientist — with respect. Having paid a seven-figure sum for the rights, Obst in turn paid screenwriter James V. Hart US$500,000 to adapt it to the screen. Ridley Scott was hired to direct for US$4 million plus 5% of the gross revenue. Jodie Foster was chosen for the lead role and was to be paid US$4 million plus another 5% of the gross.

Meanwhile, one of the losers in the auction, producer Arnold Kopelson, announced that he would make his own virus movie, to be based on a spec script by Laurence Dworet and Robert Roy Pool, writers of the unproduced screenplay *The Ultimatum*. The script was purchased for US$250,000, after which Ted Tally — Academy Award-winning screenwriter of *The Silence of the Lambs* — was paid an additional US$500,000 to give the script a "thriller edge." Kopelson even offered Scott the chance to direct his virus movie, an offer Scott angrily rejected.

Fox became concerned with the rising cost of *Hot Zone*; they wanted a strong male lead to play opposite Foster. The part of an environmentalist was rewritten as a star role for actor Robert Redford, who would be paid US$7 million plus 7% of the gross. Foster complained that her part had now been diminished and the script was again rewritten. Redford complained that now his part had been diminished. Unable to reach a compromise, Redford and Foster both left the now-US$45 million project.

Kopelson released *Outbreak* in 1995 starring Dustin Hoffman (in a role originally intended for Harrison Ford) and directed by Wolfgang Petersen. Preston criticized the producers for turning the virus into *Jaws*, but the US$50 million film was a solid international success.

Obst tried to restart *Hot Zone* with Robin Wright-Penn — hot from her Golden Globe nomination for *Forrest Gump* — and then with Emma Thompson, but the idea had lost its edge after *Outbreak*.

The truth is both darker and goofier than this. Warner Bros. had just made a successful Jodie Foster film called *Contact* with producer Lynda Obst when Lynda optioned "Crisis in The Hot Zone" and set it up — at Fox. The powers that be at Warner Bros. were furious at the perceived disloyalty and decided to commission their own film on the "Hot Zone" topic — *Outbreak*. Arnold Kopelson, who had been chasing the article as well and had delivered major hits for the studio, particularly *The Fugitive*, would produce.

The race between the studios was insane. I was in a meeting in which Kopelson, terrified he'd lose the race, asked Dworet and Pool when they could deliver a new draft. When they said it would take four weeks, he lost it. "Why should I wait four weeks for shit," he screamed, "when I can get shit in two?" The writers, who actually taped this rant, were wonderfully good humored — we all loved Arnold and understood the pressure he was under. Things later got to the point that the film actually went into production before the script was ready just so Warner Bros. could have first-out-of-the-gate bragging rights. Petersen spent a couple of weeks shooting what has to be some of the most expensive second unit footage ever produced. He was, of course, treading water, but studio chief Terry Semel was not about to lose this war.

That's the fun stuff. What's relevant to this chapter is the development process.

The article "Crisis in the Hot Zone" was about the domestic appearance of this terrifying virus that had no cure, and the first draft of the screenplay came in feeling like a "disease-of-the-week" television film. Very soft and very familiar, with an antagonist that, because it was a brainless virus, could not engage in any kind of interesting cat-and-mouse with the protagonist. It wasn't that it was bad. Act One did its job, but Act Two didn't become a "Warner movie."

It was the remarkable executive Bob Brassel who came up with the idea of modeling the film on war movies. The idea was simple: the virus would become a threat to national security. For Act 2a the virus would be contained in a small town that was quarantined with the help of the Army. In Act 2b it would mutate into something airborne that could break through the quarantine. So the race would be set — Would scientists be able find a cure for the virus before the military decided it had no choice but to obliterate the town in the hope of wiping out the virus and all who might spread it?

In this configuration, Act One needed to lay some pipe to set up the military interest in the virus, but other than that it remained essentially the same — an incurable virus from another continent takes root in the United States, the doctors who will deal with it are introduced, etc. Act Three came after the military decided it had run out of options and needed to bomb the town and the lead scientist — our protagonist — broke though the quarantine to take one last shot at finding the cure before it was too late.

Whether or not you view this premise as preposterous, this new notion for the film took a disease-of-the-week film to a war film Warner Bros. thought it could sell, with much more immediate stakes and a more obvious ticking clock. Not only that — the virus-as-antagonist was replaced with a human antagonist from the military. The fact that the role of antagonist was filled with a human being who could make decisions was much more satisfying than a dumb if implacable virus.

These decisions — how to raise the stakes, how to create an antagonist with intention, how to increase the film's scale — determine the kind of film you are making. As this example shows, they can also determine whether or not the film gets made. Because the other thing these changes did was to provide the studio's marketing department with "trailer moments." The rush to beat the Fox project meant that some mistakes were made in development that may have been preventable in a saner environment. But that doesn't detract from the wisdom of Brassel's instinct.

Both *Outbreak* and *The Fugitive* were made by Warner Bros. Both had "A" list directors and stars — Andrew Davis directed Harrison Ford and Tommy Lee Jones in *The Fugitive*, Wolfgang Petersen directed Dustin Hoffman, Renee Russo, Morgan Freeman, and Donald Sutherland in *Outbreak*. Both were high-concept films, one based on a well-known television series and one on an infamous magazine article. *Outbreak* had the additional advantage of being based on a potentially real and terrifying situation.

And yet *The Fugitive* had a worldwide gross of $370 million, whereas *Outbreak*'s worldwide gross was roughly half that — $189 million — not paltry, but certainly not what Warners had hoped for. Why?

There was a point when we were shooting the big Act Three action set piece when Dustin Hoffman told a few of us, "If you'd cast Harrison Ford for this role you'd have a huge hit." It was a funny line that probably held a grain of truth, but I don't believe it was really the big reason why one did so much better at the box office than the other.

I can tell you from having been there from the beginning of this project that every effort was made to transform a great premise into a great film. But while *The Fugitive* was a simple and elegant idea that required relatively little exposition, *Outbreak* was a whole different ballgame. The premise required huge amounts of exposition to understand — though perhaps not as much as wound up in the film. But audiences needed to understand...

- That this virus was more deadly than anything seen before.

- How the virus migrated from Africa to a small town in America.

- Why the virus became even more dangerous in that town when it mutated into something spread not just by contact but through the air.

- Why finding the host monkey (Betsy) that originally carried the virus to the United States was ultimately the only way to cure the disease.

- What the military's interest in the virus was.

- Why the military developed a cure for the original virus but then kept that a secret until after it was too late.

There was more. We called the complicated path of Betsy the monkey through the story "the Betsy trail." Brassel drew dozens of maps of the Betsy trail in story meetings, once covering an entire wall of the production office in a frenzied attempt to finally lock it down. It became a running gag — Nana Greenwald, the development executive for producer Arnold Kopelson, came up to me at the premier and joked, "Can we have a meeting about the Betsy trail?"

Added to that was the decision to add the bio warfare aspect to the plot. There were multiple reasons for this. We needed to introduce the antagonist early and to make him active. So we invented a motive for the military to stand between protagonist Gillespie and finding a cure, a secret to protect. I also think someone had the instinct that we had to make the antagonist so evil that audiences would buy his decision to torch an American city, but in my view this decision came from not trusting the film's premise — that this disease was so scary that going to any lengths to stop it would seem justified. The extra layers unnecessarily complicated an already complicated film and pushed the antagonist into moustache-twirling cartoon.

It probably seems obvious to say that the decisions we make early in the process of developing a script have far-reaching consequences. *Outbreak* is a prime example:

• The character the writers gave protagonist Gillespie was of a guy who was passionate about his work at the expense of everything else in his life, including his marriage. What that meant was that when he encountered the Motaba virus in Africa and became obsessed with the danger it represented, it was not a change from his everyday behavior. That made it challenging to get the audience invested in his mission. It might have worked if he'd been able to have a real argument with his superior, but the secret bio-weapon agenda made that difficult.

• Another difficulty: Gillespie is only afforded the opportunity to behave according to his defining quality, his predilection to defy orders and go his own way. A lot of the rest of Act Two is plot-driven, with Gillespie REACTING to events rather than initiating them. Some big issues with this second act:

- Audiences felt that the notion that our own military would torch an American town for the good of the country was preposterous. Somehow, the disease and its spread never felt credible, maybe because in Act One each previous case was halted before it could move beyond the borders of whatever village it inhabited. Interestingly, the same idea worked in *The Avengers* when the shadowy council decided to nuke New York. But *The Avengers* was a comic book film and *Outbreak* was meant to be reality. Which is to say, tone matters.

An additional lesson from *Outbreak*

One of the challenges of writing for the screen is to learn and then remember the power of visual language. There is a lot a writer can take out of their characters' mouths and put onto the screen in other ways — through action, through the use of images. No one in *Argo*, for example, needed to tell us that life in Iran was insane. We could see it.

One of the under-used allies in scripts, especially in those by new writers, is the power of actors. There was a scene in *Outbreak* that included a page-and-a-half monologue from Morgan Freeman's character. On the day the scene was shot I watched in awe as he covered the entirety of the scene with a look. Now, Freeman is an extraordinary actor and it is possible that a lesser talent in the role would not have been able to pull that off. Also, it is possible that the feat was possible only because the monologue was there first to communicate the intent of the scene to Freeman. But the lesson remains: great actors don't always need to use words to get their point across.

EXERCISES

Construct your Act Two/Continue your outline

This next group of exercises is sort of a stacked deck. You may not be able to do all of them the first time through. Some may not reveal themselves until you are into the writing. My suggestion is to work to answer as many as you can and to use the rest as guides, to be filled in as you go. This is a good way to ensure that your writing is on track.

1. Describe again the starting place for Act 2a. Remind yourself of the inciting incident and what the protagonist wants as a result. What was the first plot point, the opportunity that opened up for your protagonist? What is at stake?

2. Describe the first action your protagonist takes in order to take advantage of plot point one's opportunity. In what way is that an expression of who your protagonist is? In what way is it a risky decision?

3. Describe the midpoint, the moment that takes Act 2a's optimistic path and spins it so it leads to the low point.

4. Describe the low point. What is the worst possible thing that can happen to your protagonist short of absolute defeat?

5. Describe the second plot point, the final opportunity to get the Grail. What makes this the last opportunity for the protagonist to get what he/she wants?

6. Drop answers to 1–5 above into the beat sheet you started at the end of Chapter Three.

7. Describe the antagonist. What is his or her agenda? In what way is he or she a worthy foil for your protagonist? What is your antagonist's weak spot?

8. In what ways do the steps your protagonist takes in Act 2b seem more fraught?

9. Describe the primary emotional relationship of the film.

10. Describe your protagonist's internal journey. How does he or she change over the course of the film? When is that change manifested and how does it impact the plot?

11. Describe the ways in which the action of your Act Two is an expression of the film's theme.

12. Describe the ways in which each step the protagonist takes is driven by the character decisions you made back in Act One.

13. What is the ticking clock? Where is it introduced? How are we kept aware of it?

14. When do you reveal the secret at the heart of your film? How does that reveal energize the film?

15. Describe possible trailer moments in your Act Two.

ACT THREE:
Face/Off—A terrifying preview
and what it has to teach

Structurally, Act Three builds from the discovery of one final, desperate opportunity for the protagonist to get what he/she wants, through the final confrontation between protagonist and antagonist, and finally to a brief glimpse of the protagonist's new life. There is, of course, a raft of decisions that need to be made in constructing a screenplay's Act Three:

1. **What is this new plan?**

2. **What defines the plan as final?** In other words, why are there no more second chances?

3. **In what ways is this plan the most dangerous thing your protagonist has yet tried?**

4. **How has your protagonist changed by the time we reach the second plot point?** Is the action they are contemplating a chance they would have even considered way back when we first met them? (This question can occasionally be flipped — In an old-fashioned hero movie or in a film like *Harvey* the question is, how has the protagonist changed everyone else in the film?)

5. **What is your protagonist's state of mind at the top of Act Three?** Confident? Desperate? Fatalistic?

6. **What is your antagonist's state of mind?** Why is he/she more dangerous now than ever before?

7. **In what way is your protagonist different when the final confrontation is over? What is their life like when all is said and done?**

8. **In what way is the final showdown the ultimate expression of the film's theme?**

9. **How much do you intend to resolve?** Will all secrets be revealed, all mysteries solved? Or do you intend to take some of them to the grave, or to leave your ending ambiguous?

10. **Will the protagonist ultimately get what he or she wants?**

11. **Have you made sure that the climax of the film is worth the wait?**

12. **Are there trailer moments in Act Three?**

Analysis — Act Three of *The Fugitive*

Landing on the right Act Three for *The Fugitive* took immense amounts of work that ran most of the way through production. Part of the worry revolved around the question of how the climax could top the earlier action of the bus crash or the leap from the dam. How could the finale avoid feeling pedestrian and anti-climactic in comparison?

The problem was that, since it turned out that Dr. Charles Nichols was actually responsible for Kimble's wife's murder and that the murder was connected to the rogue pharmaceutical company, it pretty much followed that the final confrontation had to be *mano-a-mano* between Kimble and Nichols at some venue connected with the drug. In other words, it had to revolve around a standard fight-to-the-death action scene. There were only so many helicopters and crashes through skylights and cop cars careening to a halt that could be added to try to add excitement.

What saved it, ultimately, was the understanding that it was the emotional story that mattered — the decision to hold the resolution of Marshal Gerard's feelings about Kimble until the very last possible moment. Here's what we ended up with:

- Kimble leaves one-armed man Sykes' apartment to follow up on what he has learned. Would the man we met in Act One have done that? Probably not — he would have just called the cops. But he no longer trusts them — and he is too angry. His new goal is to discover who at the drug company was responsible for ordering the hit. THEREFORE...

- Believing that Lentz was the ultimate culprit, Kimble calls Nichols to tell him he knows the "truth" about Lentz — only to learn that Lentz is dead. He asks for Nichols to arrange for him to access the lab samples anyway. Nichols has no choice. BUT THEN...

- Nichols orders Sykes to kill Kimble, thereby revealing — to the audience only — the film's central secret. We are a step ahead of Kimble for the first time. Now both Gerard and Sykes are closing in on him.

- Kimble goes to the hospital and verifies the truth: the lab tests for the new drug were falsified. But he also learns the terrible fact that his buddy Nichols was behind it all. (Please notice how the filmmakers' decision to save this until now kicks up the stakes and energizes the finale.) THEREFORE...

- Kimble heads out to confront Nichols. He encounters Sykes who kills a transit cop before Kimble neutralizes him. But the dead transit cop ensures that the Chicago cops, never his friend, will now also want Kimble dead.

- Meanwhile, Gerard figures out where Kimble is headed. As part of that discovery he peruses literature from the drug company. "These pharmaceutical giants are monsters," he says, underscoring the theme that was director Andrew Davis' hook into the material.

- The finale: Kimble interrupts Nichols' moment of triumph at the convention where he is presenting the new drug. Kimble chases Nichols onto the roof where they beat on one another. Gerard gets in the middle of their fight — and at the last minute saves Kimble's life, thereby negating his earlier line, "I don't care." Kimble has won the physical battle by winning the emotional one with Gerard.

- Aftermath: Gerard joins Kimble in a cop car. It is clear from Gerard's attitude that all will be okay for Kimble — or as okay as possible given all that has happened.

It was clear from the first electrifying preview that we had gotten it right. Why did it work? The answer was that the character work done earlier in the film had been so effective that the audience was yearning for a resolution to those stories more than for pyrotechnics. The Chicago police had been biased throughout, so having them believe that Kimble had killed a transit cop ensured that the Chicago PD would want Kimble dead in the finale. The fact that Nichols seemed to have had no trouble living with his responsibility for ruining Kimble's life made us really hate him, upping the ante even more. The kicker was that the finale would also be where the bromance between Kimble and Gerard played out.

Andy Davis shot the sequence brilliantly, keeping the secret that Gerard had decided to care about Kimble's innocence until the very last minute. The finale ultimately worked (and actually seemed bigger than the bus crash) because we were so emotionally invested in the outcome, and because it had been constructed as such a perfect reflection of the film's be-true-to-yourself theme.

A third tale from the trenches —
The first preview of *Face/Off*

I have a funny history with the film *Face/Off*, written by Mike Werb and Michael Colleary. I was in one of my first Monday morning staff meetings at Warner Bros. after the weekend when everyone had read the latest draft of the script. One of the executives told his colleague who was supervising *Face/Off*, "I'm going to save your career. This is a movie about two guys who trade faces. It will never be more than a 'B' movie. Let it go." So the studio put it into turnaround.

It took years, but the film script eventually wound up at Paramount. Producer Joel Silver had been replaced with Steve Reuther and Michael Douglas. John Woo had been hired to direct John Travolta and Nicolas Cage. I started working as a development executive at Douglas-Reuther right after the film began principal photography, but it turned out that Reuther was busy trying to raise money to keep the company afloat and Michael was off shooting *The Game*. So I became their guy on set. Helping to steer this behemoth production to a safe and timely conclusion while watching John Woo set up these gigantic, operatic shots with thirteen cameras was a spectacular education. Our collaboration with the studio was nearly perfect, with production executive Nan Morales contributing in major ways.

Steve Reuther, who generally had nerves of steel, was always a mess at previews, but *Face/Off* had him practically hyperventilating. It was as though it had never occurred to him that he'd made a film that asked an audience to buy into the notion of trading faces. He was absolutely terrified by the prospect of the post-screening focus group.

For those of you unfamiliar with the film, it opens when the young son of the protagonist (John Travolta) is shot and killed by the antagonist (Nicolas Cage). There is a sequence in Act Two in which Travolta's character, wearing Cage's character's face, bonds with the bad guy's young son. This boy is nearly killed in a humongous shootout and is eventually orphaned.

So we ran this first preview and the focus group gathered. It was a remarkable moment. John Woo and his cast had totally sold the face-trading business. The audience did have one major concern, though: What happened to the young boy? It was only then that I learned — because I had not been involved in development on this project — that the original screenplay had included a final scene in which Travolta's character brought the orphaned boy home to his wife and daughter and asked their permission to adopt the kid. It had been cut to save money because people thought it unnecessary. But the audience was having none of that. Werb and Colleary's original instincts were totally vindicated.

The importance of building your audience's emotional connection to the characters and to the theme of the film cannot be overstated. There is a saying in musical theater: "You can't hum the scenery." The same goes for film. There are plenty of examples of films that have tanked at the box office despite massive special effects budgets because the audience was never emotionally invested in the film. The contrary is also true — If an audience becomes invested in a character, then you need to follow through, to reward that investment. This is important to keep in mind as you design your Act Three and decide what is important to resolve.

A brief digression about trailer moments

Having seen Anthony Minghella's film *Truly Madly Deeply,* a few of us at the studio decided we had to make Anthony's next film. I knew producer Marianne Moloney had a romantic comedy called *Mr. Wonderful* by Amy Schor and Vicki Polon. Marianne had Anthony attached to direct and the Goldwyn Company was in for half the budget. I was a junior executive at the time, but then vice presidents Courtenay Valenti and Lisa Henson got the studio to put in the other $5.5 million.

Eleven million dollars turned out to not be enough money to shoot the original Act Three finale that had protagonist Gus (Matt Dillon) chasing love interest Leonora (Annabella Sciorra) through Manhattan, with Gus' bridge-operator friends cooperating to keep her from escaping the island. Instead of petitioning for more money, Minghella wrote a beautiful, romantic, and much cheaper Act Three closer in which Gus surprised Leonora in a garden he'd decorated with zillions of white fairy lights. The scene as shot is gorgeous. But Robbie Friedman, who was head of marketing, later told me that he'd designed his campaign around the chase. He had no idea how to sell twinkle lights. So the film basically got the "Frisbee treatment" — sailing into the marketplace with no support at all.

Pay attention to the stakes. Pay attention to scale. Pay attention to the handles your screenplay gives the marketing department.

A note about writing your first draft

There is, for all practical purposes, no such thing as a screenplay that is ready to submit after only one draft, even when they are by the most successful writers. Which is to say, you will be in good company when you discover you need to revise your prized first draft. And you will discover the truth of the cliché: Writing is rewriting.

The fact that you will almost certainly need to revise is actually the good news in terms of how you approach your first draft. It allows you to make bold choices, knowing that if they don't work you can always revise.

While there are no absolutely right responses to the issues I raise in the first part of this book, there are for sure wrong ones. Wrong responses are defined as responses that are too easy, or that are not consistent with your other responses, that don't really speak to the issues or that need to be shoehorned in to work — that don't go the distance.

Knowing that, try to avoid being crippled by the need to get it right the first time out of the gate. Go for the boldest, most original ideas, and don't be scared to try something that might seem nuts. Try it with all the passion you can muster, and if it doesn't work, try something else. And look forward to the rewrite and revision phase. That's where all the fun begins.

EXERCISES

Design an Act Three that's worth the wait

1. Describe one more time the opportunity presented by the second plot point. Drop this point into the outline you have been building.

2. Describe what it is that defines the "final" plan as final. In what ways is it the most dangerous thing your protagonist has yet tried?

3. Is this final action something the protagonist would have tried when we met him/her? If not, describe the ways in which he/she has changed.

4. How much do you resolve in the final action? Is everything clear? Ambiguous? Has the protagonist won the day and gotten what he/she wanted?

5. In what way is your protagonist different when the final confrontation is over? What is their life like when all is said and done?

6. In what way is the final showdown the ultimate expression of the film's theme?

7. Describe how much you intend to resolve. Do we come away knowing the mystery at the heart of the film? Does your protagonist get everything he or she wants? Is the antagonist eliminated or reduced or simply defeated for the time being? How much do you intend to resolve?

8. Describe possible trailer moments in your Act Three.

9. Explain how the climax you intend is worth the wait. Will the reader feel that the protagonist has been pushed to his or her limits? Will an actor reading the script feel that his or her character ultimately rises above what he or she thought was possible to behave in an extraordinary way?

10. Long-term exercise: Take the basic beat sheet you have been building and start to fill in the blanks between beats to create an outline. It doesn't matter if you start by dropping in scenes you can visualize or sequences you will later break down into scenes. Different writers have different processes

for generating outlines. The classic method is with note cards and a corkboard. These can be color coded according to subplot or character or tone, depending upon what you think you need to track for the particular script you are writing. I sometimes use a program that builds organization trees. It was designed to create corporate organizational charts and meeting agendas, but I find that the graphic layout is sometimes helpful. And many of the screenwriting programs come with a note card function. The advantage of the cards, whether digital or analog, is that you can move them around as the outline takes shape.

11. Long-term exercise: Update your character bible based on what you now know about all three acts. You need to have run the series of questions outlined earlier in this book for each major character in your film. The more important the character, the more of these answers you need to have. Relatively minor characters might only have something they want, but no contradiction.

Certain screenwriting programs now come equipped with forms creating these bible pages. In addition, many writers I have worked with have found it valuable to write a short story about each of their main characters. It seems to help crystalize the answers to the important character questions. This is where you can develop backstory, quirks, motivation, etc. It is a more fluid medium than screenplay format and so sometimes it is easier to just let the ideas flow.

Many writers include their casting preferences in their character bibles. My own sense is that this can be dangerous since casting is so unpredictable — you want to be careful to not make a studio think that if they can't get Johnny Depp then they can't make the film.

12. Long-term exercise: Write your first draft, continuing to refine your outline and bible as you go. Here is an exercise

I would suggest you do periodically as you write as a way of judging if you are staying on track:

Here's a mid-quarter check-in exercise I think would be useful for everyone:

A. Write a little about the theme of your piece. (You may not know what it is yet.)

B. Write a little about the story as you now see it unfolding. Specifically, what is the journey you see your protagonist traveling? What are the few things that define him or her — that make success on their journey unlikely? What is at stake?

C. Write a little bit about the people who most impact that journey? Emotional relationships, catalysts, antagonists. Again, what FEW things define them. What is their journey?

D. What do you define as their low point?

E. Talk about what you see as the end point.

F. See if you can look at the macro steps in your story in terms of reverses. For example: A protagonist thinks she has a way to be free of her family and past, BUT THEN her father dies. THEREFORE, she has to take him to Samoa. She goes intending to drop him in the ground and get on with her life, BUT THEN her dad's wife insists on waiting for all the relatives to get there. Therefore...

G. It is okay if you can't answer all of these. But take a stab. Let's see if it helps center you in your writing? Can you get these to me by the weekend? Please let me know if that's a problem.

7 REWRITING AND REVISING:

First drafts are never as great as you think

It is almost a certainty that you will need to go back in and open up your baby more than you want. Suck it up; screenwriting is not for the faint-of-heart. But the fact that you are absolutely going to have to rewrite your first draft is also the good news, because it absolves you of the pressure to write a perfect first draft. And because, in truth, writing is rewriting. This is when you bring out the surprising truths buried in your first draft, discover the perfect words and phrases to make your characters sing and your visuals compelling.

When your screenplay is optioned by a financier, the contract will define two kinds of next steps: rewrite and polish. Imagine that you have just delivered a sculpture to the studio. Someone has told you that the overall shape is great, they love the shape, the shape could not be better — but the nose looks like the nose of a boxer, not the nose of the ballet dancer you intended. You say that you have done tons of research, there are records of ballet dancers with cauliflower noses, but the execs don't care. Not only that, but the position of the leg makes her intention unclear. Is she going to leap or run? You're not exactly sure why that's not obvious and so have to figure out what adjustments you can make with hammer and chisel that won't crack the stone and cause the entire work of art to collapse. That's a studio rewrite.

The polish step comes after everyone is happy with the "nose" and the "leg" — and often after some new reader thinks the torso is a little wide at the middle and could you fix that as well? The polish is all about getting out the rasps and rifflers, sandpaper and emery to bring out the details and colors, to add sheen to the material and subtlety to the folds. In screenwriting terms, that means to trim and tighten, to polish the dialogue and shape the paragraphs and scenes into their final form, to add last-minute detail to characters and the perfect words to descriptions.

Taken as a whole, these two steps are called development, and your contract will contemplate how many of each steps you are guaranteed, how many are optional, how much time you have for each, how much time the studio has to respond to you, and what you will get paid.

As has been mentioned earlier, buyers no longer have much of an appetite for development. There are a couple of implications of this. There is increased pressure from producers to turn around multiple drafts before the screenplay is turned in to the financer — and producers rarely want to pay for those drafts. The Writers Guild is both specific and adamant that there is no such thing as a legal free rewrite, but in reality that is a slippery slope as the producer assures you that just one more step is necessary to have it in proper shape. So it becomes a matter of negotiation as to how much free work you are willing to do to give the script its best shot.

If people are not paying for development, they are also not buying under-developed screenplays. Which means that now more than ever it pays to develop your own screenplay to as polished a version as you can before going out with it. There is a silver lining to this: You get to respond to your own notes, not the notes of someone whose agenda may be different from your own. The bad news, of course — aside from the obvious fact that no one is paying you to do this work — is that it is incumbent on you to take a good, objective look at your work, to get feedback from people you trust, and then to write really good development notes for yourself.

Polishing your script starts with a really close read. You are eventually going to send your project soaring out into the world, and like any good pilot you need to run through your pre-flight checklist.

Length? Check. Dialogue? Check. Spelling? Check...

Here, as a starting place, are...

The eight rules of the rewrite process

If the rumors are true — and they are — that there is such a place as Development Hell, then I have had my share of days playing Lucifer, presiding over a development process that was occasionally torturous for writers. Oftentimes the nightmares were avoidable. The attitude with which you approach your rewrite counts for a lot. This is the reason that, while there is some flexibility in some of the specifics in the previous chapters, there is none in these eight rules concerning the rewrite process:

Rule #1: By the time you have finished a draft you will have no objectivity left at all.

You will think you have delivered clarity, brilliance, originality. You may or may not be right, but you will neither know nor have a way to know unless you get other opinions from people you trust. You may even want to organize a table read so you can hear the piece "on its feet."

In addition to the obvious questions of "do you like it?" and "did it make you laugh/cry/pee with fear?" and "What did and did not work?" there are some issues for which fresh eyes can be particularly useful:

- Your script should break roughly into quarters and, depending upon genre, should run from 95 to 125 pages. A first act longer than 30 pages or a script that is much longer or much shorter usually has major structural issues that need to be resolved. So you will have to go back and see what can be cut or combined. Extra eyes helping you figure out what you could lose can be very helpful.

- You want to make sure that you don't drop important characters or subplots for too long.

- You want to make sure the piece has musical dynamics, by which I mean that it has variations of rhythm and intensity, of highs and lows. So asking where people got bored — or doing a table read and seeing where you get bored — can also be incredibly useful.

• When your friends read your script through, does it feel to them like you really know your subject? Does it feel like you've fudged details? The line, "Write what you know," should not be taken as reductive; it works as well to learn your subject so that by the time you finish your research you are writing what you know. One way or the other you have to know every detail of the world you are creating. Do your readers get this sense from your script?

• When they read your script through, is it clear that you know your intention, that you have been clear about what your film is about? A war of ideas as embodied in the characters is its own kind of drama and makes the most mundane films into an interesting dialectic. *Thelma & Louise* was just a buddy road movie but for the really interesting battle between Thelma's yen for freedom and its impossibility in her circumstances. But if you or your readers can't tell someone what your script is about in a line or two describing story and a line or two describing theme, then you are probably in trouble.

Rule #2: As my former boss Steve Reuther used to say, "If enough people tell you you're drunk, sit down."

Ruthless honesty about whether or not your intentions are actually landing on the page is required, and you have to be willing and able to hear the critique. It is never true that if you believe something is working and no one else is getting it, it is because all of your readers are idiots. If you get consistent feedback that something is not working, it is because something needs fixing.

Knowing what it is that needs fixing and how to make that fix are among the key skills you need to develop. The trick to not losing your mind in the process is to remember that while you are required to listen to the essence of other people's notes, you are not even the tiniest bit obligated to take anyone's specific suggestions — which will be wrong

99% of the time in any case. Go back, figure out why your ideas aren't landing, re-work your outline, and rewrite. And remember Dede Allen's edict: The problem with a scene is often found in the scenes meant to set up the offending scene, not in the scene itself.

The development process can for sure be bruising. There is a writer/director with whom I used to work who, upon receiving a set of notes from me, would send back an equally long email detailing all the things justifying his conclusion that I was a philistine. He actually discusses these exchanges in the "additional materials" section of the film he made based on the screenplay we worked on together. We still laugh about the email he forgot to mention, the one he sent me apologizing for all the vitriol and thanking me for making his script better. This is not my way of tooting my own horn. My point is that sometimes unwanted feedback can actually be valuable. The flip side of this is that studio executives actually keep some version of the life's-too-short list of writers with whom they never want to work. So it is a good idea to practice how to deal with notes you may not want to hear.

Rule #3: You can't cut corners.

One of my favorite assignments when I was at Warner Bros. was working with legendary animation director Chuck Jones on a new Road Runner cartoon. Chuck carried a deep disgust for the two executives he reported to, Leon Schlesinger and Ray Katz. He used to tell this great tale about the day Leon and Ray came to the studio known as "Termite Terrace" to announce that times were tough and the artists had to start cutting corners. The next time they visited they discovered that the animators had taken a saw and cut the corners off all their desks. A fantastic prank that pretty much sums up my own feeling about the wisdom of cutting corners during the writing process. Don't do it. You'll pay for it eventually.

Rule #4: Know what you're writing about.

One of my students discovered this quote from director/producer Sydney Pollack. "Trivial as it may sound," Pollack said, "it's important to me to be able to describe the heart of a film simply and evocatively in order to test each scene, character, and development against that idea." One of your chief rewrite tasks is to lift yourself out of the fog of celebration at having gotten through a draft and dig back in as if you're reading your own work for the first time in order to discover the heart of your piece. More on this later.

Rule #5: Learn the rules of screenwriting.

Learn them so well that you can forget them. Learn them so well that they become second nature, and then execute on them with as much rigor and imagination as you can manage.

William Goldman famously wrote about screenwriting that if you don't want to collaborate, become a novelist. I would add that if you are rule-averse, find a different career entirely. You don't have to hit the beats in the same way as everyone else, but you do have to hit them. There is great beauty and power and variation inside the rigid demands of screenwriting. Or, perhaps music is a better analogy. Learning your scales does not mean you get up and perform those scales. It means that the knowledge you gain with musical form and structure informs what you play and gives you the means to improvise inside that.

Rule #6: Do not start your rewrite without an outline and character bible.

Many writers take the position that, since first drafts need to develop organically as the writing proceeds, outlines and character bibles are somewhere between a waste of time and impossible to write. This is sometimes okay. First drafts can indeed be where a writer throws his or her ideas onto a page — although the tradeoff is frequently that second drafts need lots of adjustments.

After the first draft, a whole new discipline sets in. Your goal from here on out is to tease out what is important from what you threw onto the page and shape that into a tight, coherent screenplay. This book poses a raft of decisions you need to have made before you can deliver a great script. While you don't necessarily have to have all the answers before you start your first draft, you ABSOLUTELY need to have them before you start your rewrite. And you need to use those answers as a guide to a complete outline and character bible.

Rule #7: If it's too hard to fix, it might be time to re-think.

There are a couple of aspects to this rule. A plot that is too complicated will often collapse of its own weight. Beyond that, if a story problem becomes too difficult to solve, if it becomes a wildly complicated exercise to make it work, then chances are you have somehow gotten off track.

There is actually a scientific basis for this rule. Jim Holt, in his marvelous tract *Why Does the World Exist? — An Existential Detective Story*, tells us,

> Mathematical beauty has time and again proved to be a reliable guide to physical truth, even in the absence of empirical evidence. "You can recognize truth by its beauty and simplicity," said [physicist] Richard Feynman. "When you get it right, it is obvious that it is right."[3]

Conversely, when you get it wrong it starts to be obvious by the degree of difficulty you find in getting it to work. An example might be Warner Bros. excruciating effort to develop a new Superman movie. The character had a tragic flaw, which was that he had no flaw. His only weakness was his susceptibility to Kryptonite. Such a nearly perfect character held little appeal for modern audiences. It apparently took David Goyer and Christopher Nolan to figure out that the original version of the character was simply not going to work. So they created a prequel in which the character had a defining contradiction. As of this writing, *Man of Steel* is still in post production so I have no idea how well the new formula works. But the decision to break away from what had become an insoluble problem and try something different got the project past years of development hell.

One final word in this section: There is a corollary to this rule that concerns the need to keep your script from getting too complicated.

---

3 *Why Does the World Exist? — An Existential Detective Story* by Jim Holt. Liveright Publishing Corporation, New York, 2012. Page 172.

A fine line you need to walk as a screenwriter is that you must give the impression that you know everything there is to know about the world you are writing about and the characters who inhabit it, but you need to choose from that enormous storehouse of information exactly the right details to clearly define that world and those characters without overwhelming your readers. One of the contradictions of screenwriting is that although you need to know so much, you need to boil your knowledge down to the essentials.

A screenplay is an incredibly condensed form that requires a certain level of simplicity. As discussed elsewhere, a single set of contradictory characteristics is often all you need to create a wonderfully compelling protagonist whose struggles will drive a film. Not only that: adding very much more to that mix will tend to befoul your story and sink clarity in a sea of unnecessary complication.

Interestingly, there is now research into the workings of the brain that underscores these points about screenwriting — and, indeed, about writing in general. It turns out that there are filters that only allow "appropriate" input to reach the higher brain. This is not the right venue in which to get into long explanations of how this all works, but there are conclusions from the research that are well worth remembering:

- The first filter, like a good doorman at a trendy club, only wants to allow novelty, surprise, color, and unexpected or curious events through. This should be translated as an edict against writing what you've seen before and for digging in to discover what is unique in your own story.

- When the reader feels stressed, a second brain filter goes into survival mode and diverts what is being input away from the thinking brain and into the more primitive fight/flight center. Confusion and boredom are both known to cause this kind of stress and can lead a reader to hurl a screenplay into the huge pile of scripts they will either resent or refuse to finish. Writer Steve Almond, in his tiny book (41 pages) of brilliant essays on writing called *This Won't Take But a Minute, Honey*, has a rule he calls The Hippocratic Oath of Writing: "Never confuse the reader." It is a great foundational rule on which to build your methodology for getting the right answer to the question, "Is it a film?" Never confuse the reader.

Rule #8: Remember that your job is to entertain.

I know this last one seems weird, but it is sort of a catch-all for a whole lot of what I am writing about. The rules of screenwriting really come from the rules of dramatic structure as created by the ancient Greeks. There is, of course, some stuff in this book not known to the Greeks — they probably didn't worry much about trailer moments — but we still use much of what they discovered about telling stories in ways that engage an audience, about creating compelling characters with whom an audience can identify, and about pushing characters to be human and unique and iconic all at the same time.

The most important legacy of these Greek playwrights is this: If there is no dramatic tension, there is no entertainment. Even when you feel you have something terribly important to say, that theme needs to be buried inside entertainment. As Pete Dexter wrote in his October 2, 2011, *New York Times* "Book Review" piece about Jim Harrison's novel *The Great Leader*, "To enlighten and to entertain, what else is there? And while good books — even so-so books — serve both functions, if you ever have to choose one over the other, keep in mind that a book that entertains without enlightening can still be a guilty pleasure, but a book that enlightens without entertaining is algebra." Screenwriters with serious intent should keep this in mind.

The clearest clues that you have a ways to go

It is not so easy to either recognize or hear about weaknesses in your own first draft. But there are a couple of clear signs that where you're headed next is a rewrite and not a polish.

Log lines: It may seem like I'm raising the specter of log lines late in the book. Shouldn't you have one before you start writing? Well, of course it would be best. Knowing where you're headed always makes getting there easier and more efficient. But screenplays tend to morph as characters take on lives of their own and start to dictate where your story is headed.

"Log line" is sort of a misnomer because it implies that you should be able to describe your screenplay in a single line. The truth, as with so much else in this book, is that there is some flexibility in this. But in general you should be able to explain your story and central conflict in at most a few lines. The extent of difficulty you have in accomplishing this is one measure of how much work remains to be done. If you can't give a clear, succinct sense of the journey of the script, then it is almost certain that it is either too complicated (as opposed to complex) or too unfocused. Even complex films are built around a fairly simple spine. For the most part, the object is to take your audience on one person's journey as he or she chases one very specific desire. To attempt much more than that is usually an exercise in confusion in which the audience doesn't know what story to attach to. If you can't identify and describe that journey, then chances are your script will feel flabby at best and meander all over the map at worst. Focus is key, and one reflection that you have your project in focus is a great log line.

Log lines are not the same as marketing tag lines. Log lines are distilled versions of your film. The best log lines usually indicate both your protagonist's main character contradiction and the plot that brings that contradiction to the level of crisis. Some examples:

Amadeus: In his youth, Antonio Salieri wanted to be a great composer so badly he made a pact with God in which he traded servitude for talent, but as soon as he hears the music of Wolfgang Amadeus Mozart he realizes that God has betrayed him and given the gift instead to this vulgar and Godless young man. Salieri vows to destroy the younger composer, and takes them both down in the process.

The Fugitive: Falsely accused of murder, Richard Kimble wants to find his wife's real killer, but his need to do the right thing in every situation no matter how dangerous leaves a string of clues that lead the relentless U.S. Marshall Gerard ever closer to capturing him.

Avatar: Jake Sully wants the use of his legs back so badly he is willing to make a deal with the powers of corporate greed to help steal an innocent race's resources, but his need to be a genuine hero on the side of good ultimately pits him against his own race.

Please notice that in each log line the protagonist is the active character. The core stress points in the story are clear, as are the traits and contradictions that make the roles interesting. The harder it is to reduce your film to a sentence or two, the more likely it is that you haven't found its real through line.

A great logline provides a steady platform and a clear track over which to propel your story. So long as your scenes stay on this track your story can't go too far astray.

Statement of theme: The same thing I said about log lines applies to themes. You have to be able to provide a clear line describing what your film is about, what it has to say. The reasons are similar — if you know what it is you are trying to say, then you have a guide against which to measure each scene and every decision your characters make. Your characters' actions, both active and reactive, are all based in decisions they make, and those decisions need to be expressions of the film's theme. For those of you who are mathematically inclined, one way to think about a screenplay is as a proof. Someplace in Act One you state the premise you are trying to prove. Each movement that follows is in some way a step in executing that proof.

Be your own script whisperer: Discovering your screenplay's hidden truth

How do you discover the deeper truth in your own writing? It is remarkable how often I read a writer's work and see some truly profound underpinning of which the student is utterly unaware. This makes sense on some level. Think of all the times literary critics write of the deeper meaning of a book only to have the author respond, "That was far from intentional." But screenwriting is weird — scripts are so distilled that consistency and fealty to a specific idea can be make-or-break stuff.

When I was working toward my own MFA I discovered a methodology for doing my critical writing. I would choose a book because it seemed somehow relevant to my thesis, but I harbored no expectations or thesis to prove when I started reading. I would read until the alchemical moment when the golden core of the book would reveal itself. Sometimes it was a phrase, sometimes an image, sometimes a technique — but it always happened. That's when I knew what to write about.

So the question is, can a screenwriter, who after completing a first draft will have absolutely no objectivity at all, find a way to accomplish that kind of unbiased reading of his or her own work? I think this is one of those places where having trusted second readers take a look at your work and telling you what they took from it can be really valuable. Not that you are required to buy into their take. But if you choose wisely, they will point you in interesting directions and you can go back in and look for ways to strengthen that core.

Or not. In the eventuality that neither they nor you can give a precise description of what the script is about, then you are up against a different sort of a problem. If neither you nor your readers can find a concise meaning or point of view, then your task is to go back in and really try to understand why you were drawn to the material in the first place. Most of you are writing because you have something to say. At some point in your process your own creations will take on a life of their own and whisper hints that you — sometimes unconsciously — put on the page. But for many writers it is as if their muses are writing them love letters in invisible ink. They have to read and re-read their own work until the intensity of their reading acts like the candle in the invisible ink experiments, heating the paper until the message comes through. This process can be painstaking, but the rewards of the treasure hunt can be enormous.

Making peace with ceding control
to your own subconscious

I have a student named Jay who wrote a wonderful first draft of a script based on the true story of a tragedy that took place in Iran. Jay had first written this piece as a play that was produced in London. His chief interest was in the story of the two Iranian boys at the center of the story — he'd written the piece to tell their story. But when he adapted the piece for film a producer told him that he needed a role for an American star if he wanted to get the film financed. So he invented a young American woman through whose eyes we see the story unfold. As a child, this woman lost her single mother in 9/11; when the film opens she is in her early twenties and requires a heart transplant to survive. Her self-destructive lifestyle means that she has fallen off the list of people approved for transplants — and her Persian doctor offers her a chance for survival if she will pay him directly and travel with him to Iran — the place in the world she would least like to go — for the surgery.

The thing that happened in the writing was that this character took on a life of her own. She became the protagonist. Jay had unwittingly created a fantastic vehicle for telling his story that was completely invisible to him. He was terrified that her story would overshadow that of the boys, but his leading lady was telling him that the way to present that story was to focus on her transformation and redemption as she bore witness to the events that interested Jay. She was a woman whose heart was literally sick but also scarred by grief and prejudice, and by bearing witness to the tragedy she could heal both her literal and figurative heart. It was a fascinating process to get him to see what he himself had put on the page. The truth is, at some point he'd ceased being the active writer and started being the channel to his own characters, and his protagonist's words and import took him totally by surprise. There was Truth in his screenplay that went far beyond what he'd originally intended.

In this process, I acted as lead investigator for Jay in unearthing the true source of the power of his script, but in truth the clues were there for him to read once he washed his mind of the fear that he'd lost his way. Quite the opposite was true.

What were those clues?

• The protagonist had lost her mother in 9/11.

• She'd grown into a totally self-destructive woman, an indication of unresolved grief and rage.

• She expressed horror at the prospect of traveling to Iran and mistrust of her Persian doctor, both expressions of prejudice.

• She calmed her rage and accepted that suffering is universal and nothing is as black and white as it seems as a result of her time in Iran and her involvement in the boys' story.

These do not seem like subtle hints about the nature of her story. The trick in this case was in recognizing that this character had become both the protagonist and the audience's eyes into the story Jay wanted to tell. And the key to that came when Jay saw that she in fact made the greatest internal journey. This was not an easy call. The boys whose story first caught Jay's attention went from innocent belief that they could determine their own futures to victims of a corrupt and prejudiced system that executed them for their dreams. That's a pretty major journey. But the woman Jay had created went from a sort of global, self-destructive hatred that stemmed from an act of horror we'd all shared to life-affirming compassion. It was the more universal journey and a story that could include and highlight the story of the boys.

Finding that core idea and staying true to it is how you raise above pure craft to deliver something memorable. Look, for example, at the way that theme defined the films *The Avengers* and *Driving Miss Daisy*, two very different films that made stunning connections with their audiences.

The Avengers' theme is this: In a world where forces have been unleashed that wish to destroy or enslave us, salvation can only come from working together. Look at how that solid idea defines the incredibly effective trailer. "You were made to be ruled," antagonist Loki tells us. "In the end, it will be every man for himself." Samuel Jackson's character then reveals his plan to save the day: "Bring together a group of remarkable people so that when we need them, they could fight the battles we never could." And then "Iron Man" Tony Stark states the character dilemma that drives the film, "I don't play well with others." This is the weakness amongst the heroes that Loki tries to exploit; it is what Jackson's character manipulates to overcome the forces of evil. And we can tell from the trailer that there is a coherent, compelling, timely — and fun — story awaiting us in the theaters.

Driving Miss Daisy by Alfred Uhry was made for under ten million dollars — which even adjusting for inflation was probably less than the catering budget for *The Avengers* — and had a worldwide gross of $145 million. This was in 1989 and the film had just won the Best Picture Oscar when I was hired as a reader at Warner Bros. The studio hadn't made the film; this was a negative pick-up. For some reason, president of production Bruce Berman wanted to interview me before my hire was finalized. "Congratulations on the Oscar," I said as we shook hands. "I guess this'll change things here at the studio. I mean, percentage-wise it has to be one of the all-time most profitable films, and it's winning awards."

"Thanks," Bruce said. "But it won't change a thing. We'd still never make that film."

So there you have it. Warner Bros. is always going to make "Warner films." But that film still got made, still found a huge audience. The script got Bruce Beresford to direct and it got the sublime Jessica Tandy and Morgan Freeman to play the leads. Why? I mean, why did that tiny script get such a resounding "Yes!" to the question "Is it a movie?" No one knows the whole answer — I'd be lying if I said I did. But watch the trailer on YouTube (*http://www.youtube.com/watch?v=BR0oZ2pnhyg*). This is a film that clearly knew what it was about. Freeman says, "I'm just the back of a neck you look at when you're going wherever you've got to go. I'm a man." You can see the trailer wrap around that theme and, if you go back and watch the movie, you can see the whole film wrapped around it.

I want to end this section by examining the trailer for *Argo* (*http://www. youtube.com/watch?v=5ESR382L7Wo*). I love this trailer. Why? Because I love the line, "This is the best bad idea we have, sir." Because I love the theme that "We're responsible for these people."

But mostly, I love it because of the importance it gives to good story. "You really believe your little story will make a difference when there's a gun to our head?" one of the hostages asks Ben Affleck's character. He replies, "I think my little story is the only thing between you and a gun to your head."

As a screenwriter, that needs to be your point of view about your story. You're selling it to an angry mob of viewers who have overpaid for the privilege of seeing your movie. Your life as a screenwriter depends upon winning their trust — which is to say, on telling the Truth. Your characters, your own creations, will tell you that Truth if you are willing to listen.

How to sabotage your own rewrite — Self-destructive writers I have known

I once had a student to whom I gave the note that a particular character in his screenplay was behaving in a way that was entirely inconsistent with what he'd set up. "That's what everyone keeps telling me," he wrote back. "No one is getting what I mean..." This student's excuse for why he didn't need to do any work on the script was that none of us who were reading his work were getting it. Translation: We were all morons or we'd understand what he'd intended.

This was the very definition of the self-destructive writer. They come in all sorts of varieties. There are those who flat-out refuse to do any work on their scripts. There are the more passive-aggressive ones who make minimal, only-on-the-surface changes. And there are the ones who rant and rail and scream, but who finally do the work. I much prefer the latter group. The discussion, even when it becomes unpleasant, almost always leads to better solutions than those suggested in my notes. It is the utter refusals or passive-aggressive virtual refusals whose projects invariably fail.

After you have read and re-read — and then re-re-read — your script, after you have gotten all the feedback you can stomach, you will need to dive back in and start the re-write process. There is no denying that this is both daunting and potentially discouraging, because at this point you literally need to go back to the beginning and run the same checklist that you ran when you started the draft — only this time what you are looking for is how thoroughly the draft speaks to each issue and where there might be leaks in an otherwise watertight story. Having been down this road once, it can be difficult to re-set and do it again. Trust me on this. It will be worth the pain.

EXERCISES

Getting ready for your rewrite

These exercises are broken into two parts, the first a preparation for the second.

1. Write a new paragraph describing the reason you wrote this particular screenplay. Try to recall what it was about the story and characters that particularly interested you. What discoveries have you made along the way that have either changed or deepened those reasons. What is it that particularly interests you about your story or characters now?

2. Where are your characters' actions diverging from your original intent? Look to see where their behavior is an expression of their character and where it might feel forced to fit your original intent. Look to see where there might be implied storylines that don't feel complete.

3. Give your draft to some trusted friends to read. Assemble their feedback. Are there common threads? Describe them? Write a

little bit about what you think the source of those issues might be. Are there things that you intended that do not seem to be landing on the page for your readers? Make a separate list of your readers' suggestions for fixes. Do not yet make a judgment call on which of those suggestions you might want to take.

4. Write a log line and statement of theme for your screenplay. Where is your piece too fuzzy or too complicated to describe succinctly?

5. Write a brief biography of your protagonist. Give a little bit of backstory and a description of who he or she is when we meet them. What's right with their life? What's wrong with it? Is there something they are missing? Something without which life would be unbearable? Describe. Do the same for your antagonist. For the object of the key emotional relationship.

Below you will find a compilation and extension of exercises you have seen before. But taken together and answered after you have finished a draft, they form a checklist that can help you identify the weak spots in your script and therefore the areas of concentration for your rewrite. You can also use as a final test to make sure you are ready to start your first draft or as a way of locating the cause for why you might be stuck mid-draft.

The places where your answers seem fuzzy or incomplete will form the basis for your rewrite notes. At this point I think it is important to separate out the rewrite notes from the polish notes. The process can be needlessly overwhelming if you try to tackle everything at once. If you have major structural issues, then doing a dialogue polish is pointless. Why revise a scene that may not survive the rewrite? You want to save yourself as many steps as you can, to be as efficient as possible. One of the key pitfalls into Development Hell is the kind of fatigue that cripples weightlifters after too many repetitions. Do the big stuff first, and then move on to the fine tuning.

1. Describe the film's place, era, and time frame. Do those elements impact the story? If so, how?

2. Describe the film's tone and genre. How is genre communicated in Act One?

3. Describe your protagonist's life before the plot sets in. What is it that he or she values most about that life? What story do you set in motion? This is the story that will be interrupted by the inciting incident.

4. Is there a clear inciting incident? Exactly how does that put the protagonist in a position where they can't go back to life as it was? How does it create a crisis in their life? What is the new thing that they *must* have as a result? Remember, this is the beat that answers the story question, "Why now?"

5. What is the first plot point? Exactly how does it provide an opportunity to resolve the crisis raised by the inciting incident? What is it about that opportunity that is risky for the protagonist — why does he or she hesitate to take that opportunity?

6. What is the character contradiction that will make this journey challenging? What is the character flaw that will define the character's internal journey? In *Avatar*, these are the same thing — Jake Sully was a warrior willing to make a deal with the devil in order to regain the use of his leg, but he turned out to have the heart of a hero. In *The King's Speech*, the protagonist was born to public life but was cursed with an extreme stutter. His internal journey was to unearth and deal with his own terrible childhood. In *Erin Brockovich*, Erin needed to take on corporate America but had no legal training. Her internal journey brought her the self-confidence she needed in order to accomplish what she wanted.

7. What is the theme of your film? Where is it stated in Act One? How is it expressed through the actions of the protagonist?

8. Have you tried to introduce too many characters at once? Is each one distinct enough that the story will be easy to follow?

9. What is the central secret of the film? How have you set that up in Act One? Where do you reveal it? What is the impact of that reveal on your protagonist?

10. What is the central emotional relationship of the film and how does it track through your film? Where do you introduce that relationship?

11. Is there a clear moment when the protagonist *decides* to take the opportunity offered by the first plot point?

12. What and who stands in the protagonist's way of getting what he/she wants? What does the antagonist want? What is his or her weak spot? Remember that the antagonist must be something external that can maneuver and escalate his or her efforts to thwart the protagonist.

13. How is the conflict between want and need resolved over the course of the film? Does the protagonist ever have a revelation that moves him or her toward that resolution? How does that revelation help energize the story and accelerate it toward its conclusion?

14. Is the first half of Act Two a series of reversals in which things seem to go pretty well for the protagonist? Is the antagonist becoming increasingly frustrated? Is each scene in a given subplot connected by either "BUT THEN..." or "THEREFORE..."?

15. What is the midpoint that spins things around such that things start to look increasingly dire for the protagonist? Describe the change.

16. Describe the way in which things look increasingly dire for the protagonist.

17. Describe the low point where it looks like all is lost for the protagonist.

18. Describe the second plot point that presents the protagonist with one final, desperate opportunity. What is it that opens up that opportunity? In other words, is your protagonist able to take advantage of this opportunity because of some change he or she has undergone, or because of something they have discovered? Is that moment of change or discovery clear?

19. What defines the protagonist's last opportunity as final? In what ways is it the most dangerous thing your protagonist has yet tried?

20. Does the climax match the scale of the film? Does it test the protagonist to his or her full potential? Does it resolve all that needs to be resolved?

21. Have you defined your target audience? Are you consistent in your approach to that audience?

22. Have you created a compelling ticking clock?

23. In what way is your protagonist different when the final confrontation is over? What is their life like when all is said and done?

THE POLISH:
Wordsmithing your screenplay

We are at the final step of the process, though it is more than likely that you will need to take more than one pass through this step to finally get it right. There are so many elements that go into a great script. There are the obvious ones — structure, character, dialogue, etc. And then there are the less obvious things — word choice, paragraph shape, etc. These less obvious things together with some final shaping are the stuff of the polish step.

When are you ready to polish?

The truth is, you will more than likely polish your screenplay every time you go through it, fixing a word or a phrase or a line of dialogue. But THE polish starts when all of the heavy lifting is done, when your screenplay's structure holds water and most of the invention is over. When you can give clear responses to all of the questions in the previous chapters' exercises. The goal now is to make your script the most readable and compelling version of itself it can be.

Word choice — the poetry of screenwriting

A large part of the goal of the polish is to hone your language, both in dialogue and description, so that it is saying exactly what you want it to say in the most eloquent and evocative way possible. There is a fine line to walk here: A screenplay is not a literary work and the last thing you want is for long paragraphs of flowing description to slow down the read. You are writing primarily for an audience that is plowing through piles of scripts. You don't want them to be screaming, "Get to the point!" or "You're NOT the director!" You want your language to convey momentum, energy, tension, visuals, etc.

How do you accomplish that? I might start by reading William Goldman's screenplay for *Butch Cassidy and the Sundance Kid* for a lesson in writing motion. In fact, read as many screenplays as you can. If you are just starting off, you need to absorb the strange rhythm of screenwriting, to learn how other writers handle the issues of their particular script.

Screenwriting, like all other forms of writing, is first and foremost a series of decisions. What's the right word? What is it that I need to accomplish in this scene? What out of all the things I could describe in this scene is THE thing that will tell the reader what I need him/her to know? Where should I break my paragraphs? In these regards there are valuable lessons to be learned from other genres.

For example, I have my classes read a personal essay by Pulitzer Prize winner Annie Dillard called "Total Eclipse."[4] Of her own process, Dillard writes about one novel that started out at 1,200 pages but ended up "pure and plain," losing some of her favorite passages in her process of carving back to the core.

So that's one huge lesson: Include only what's necessary. Lose the redundant, the sloppy, the unnecessary.

The essay "Total Eclipse" is Dillard's attempt to evoke the terrifying two minutes she spent as an observer of a total solar eclipse, using her trip to Yakima, Washington, and various random thoughts to try to put the experience — clearly in some ways beyond words — into words. Here is how she opens:

> It had been like dying, that sliding down the mountain pass.
> It had been like the death of someone, irrational, that sliding
> down the mountain pass and into the region of dread. It was
> like slipping into fever, or falling down that hole in sleep

4 *Teaching a Stone to Talk — Expeditions and Encounters.* HarperPerennial, New York. 1982. Pages 9–28.

from which you wake yourself whimpering. We had crossed the mountain that day, and now we were at a strange place, a hotel in central Washington in a town near Yakima. The eclipse we had traveled to see would occur early the next morning.

Look what Dillard does. She's traveling to see an eclipse, we know that from the title, it seems sort of mundane — yet the first words she chooses are, "It had been like dying, that sliding down the mountain pass and into the region of dread." She's writing from the future, she's remembering she'd ventured into some literal hell. We know right from the start that she is about to experience a living near-death. If that was a sentence in a screenplay I would know so much about the tone of what's coming. I'd know where I was headed. And notice the sense of suspense created by the word "strange," placed just so to give the hotel a horror-movie sheen.

Dillard goes on to describe her motel room:

> I lay in bed. My husband Gary was reading beside me. I lay in bed and looked at the painting on the hotel room wall. It was a print of a detailed and lifelike painting of a smiling clown's head, made out of vegetables. It was a painting of the sort which you do not intend to look at, and which, alas, you never forget. Some tasteless fate presses it upon you, it becomes part of the complex interior junk you carry with you wherever you go. Two years have passed since the total eclipse of which I write. During those years I have forgotten, I assume, a great many things I wanted to remember but I have never forgotten that clown painting or its lunatic setting in that old hotel.

Look at the detail she chooses to give us. That terrible painting of a clown assembled from vegetables. She tells us she was in bed with her husband. In fact she repeats that information, as though to remind herself and emphasize to us how normal and safe everything felt. And then she gives us that hideous painting, one of the few things that stuck in her memory from that night. It was normal, it was cheap, it was the product of some false artistic striving — and, as we find out later in the essay, Dillard was about to face God. The contrast does so much to anchor us to "normal" as it must have for her when the world was vanishing beneath the seemingly onrushing, darkening sun. And emphasizing the mundane will help her express the extraordinary by contrast. She could have described the bed linens, the room color, the cheap rug, the view out the window — but she chose that one detail and it told us everything we needed to know.

These are the kinds of choices you have to make in your screenplay. You could indeed tell us about the color of the walls and the smell of the sheets, the condition of the carpet and the shape of the lamps — and we, the readers of your script, would not be impressed by the richness of your imagination and the clarity with which you see the room. We'd want to hunt you down for overwhelming us with detail. Choose the one detail that tells us everything we need to know.

Shaping your paragraphs

I recently read Tony Kushner's *Lincoln* screenplay. A close study shows that its fluidity has a lot to do with the way he organizes and shapes his paragraphs of description and action. It's all about economy, saying as much as possible with as few words as possible; and about keeping thoughts and actions from leaking onto one another — keeping the space around them clean so it is easy to follow the movement of the story. I started to think of each paragraph as a frame of film moving through the projector's gate, and of the content of that paragraph as the moment being framed. The paragraphs are built around what is most important to bring center frame, to bring out, to highlight the point of the scene. Background details are chosen — and limited to — those things that might give us the most important information as we move through the scene. If each scene is a step through the story, each paragraph is a step through the scene. Taken together, they should form discreet "stills" that pull us through the scene.

Below is an excerpt from Kushner's script — except I have removed all dialogue from it. The scenes describe a nightmare Lincoln has, followed by an excerpt from the scene in which he tells his wife Mary about it. Pay careful attention to where he breaks each paragraph...

EXT. A SHIP AT SEA — NIGHT

A huge, dark, strange-looking steamship, part wood and part iron, turreted like a giant ironclad monitor, is plowing through the choppy black waters of an open sea. **[This paragraph has the sole function of setting the scene.]**

Lincoln is alone, in darkness, on the deck, which has no railing, open to the sea. The ship's tearing through rough water, but there's little pitching, wind or spray. The deck is dominated by the immense black gunnery turret. **[This one places Lincoln on the ship and paints a picture of the storm he faces.]**

Lincoln stares out towards a barely discernible horizon, indicated by a weird, flickering, leaden glow, which appears to recede faster than the fast-approaching ship. **[Note that Kushner started a new paragraph to tell us what Lincoln sees. So these three paragraphs give us setting, then character, then his POV. Three discreet ideas in three discreet paragraphs.]**

INT. MARY'S BOUDOIR, SECOND FLOOR OF THE WHITE HOUSE — NIGHT

The room's cozy, attractive, cluttered, part dressmaker's workshop, part repository of Mary's endless purchases: clothing, fabrics, knicknacks, carpets. Books everywhere. **[Again, note that he opens this new scene with setting.]**

Lincoln reclines on a French chair, too small
for his lengthy frame. He's in shirtsleeves,
vest unbuttoned and tie unknotted, shoeless. He
has an open folio filled with documents on his
lap. [**Now he places Lincoln in the scene…**]

MARY LINCOLN sits opposite, in a nightgown,
housecoat and night cap. She watches him in her
vanity mirror. [**…now he places Mary in it…**]

She looks frightened. [**…and now he tells us her
state of mind.**]

This way of looking at how a page is laid out is not always part of the literature on screenwriting, but it can make a huge difference in how people view your script. It demonstrates an understanding of the way things move in and out of focus in a scene, in and out of the foreground, so that the scene is easiest to traverse. If discreet parts of a scene feel all jumbled together, then the screenplay starts to feel jumbled, and for people who read scripts day in and day out, it translates as a cue that the writer doesn't really have control of his or her material.

The dialogue polish

When the great writer John Updike died, the *Los Angeles Times* obituary (January 28, 2009, section D page 2) included this quote from a piece of his about baseball:

> The ball climbed on a diagonal line into the vast volume of air over center field. From my angle, behind third base, the ball seemed less an object in flight than the tip of a towering motionless construct, like the Eiffel Tower or the Tappan Zee Bridge. It was in the books while it was still in the sky.

To me, this is breathtaking writing. "It was in the books while it was still in the sky…" How does someone come up with a line like that? I was studying in Goddard College's creative writing program at the time Updike died and asked two of my writing teachers what they would tell their students about how one achieves that kind of music. Here are their responses:

"No one but Updike can write an Updike sentence, of course. I think the answer is that one must engage so obsessively with one's own sentences that they ultimately, with relentless practice, become their own thing, which in turn becomes your style. This part of it is up to the writer himself/herself."

Victoria Nelson

"I'd have your students listen to books (in their chosen genre/style) on tape before they write. Word choices and tonal inflections pop up that can be inspiring — or warning."

Aimee Liu

The answer boils down to the same thing I'd learned from the Tim Burton installation: You have to study the masters, you have to absorb the world swirling around you. You have to listen to films in the genre you are writing in. And then you have to practice and practice and practice capturing it and then practice some more to make it your own.

But there are some questions that you can and should ask yourself as you are reading your own dialogue:

1. **Does the dialogue match the character?** Is the character educated? Where? Do they have an attitude? Are they shy? Aggressive? Is that captured in how they speak?

2. **Have you maximized the use of subtext and action to express the themes and ideas of your film?** Put another way, have you eliminated as much on-the-nose exposition as possible? There is a character that has a variety of names but who makes unexpected appearances in too many screenplays and who is hated in all of his guises. I call him "Moishe the Explainer." Moishe the Explainer is someone you want to banish from your script to the greatest extent possible.

We have already discussed the use of action to tell us all about the character of Richard Kimble. Another example: In *Arthur* — the 1981 original, written and directed by Steve Gordon — there is a glorious scene when Arthur's elderly butler Hobson (John Gielgud) is dying and Arthur (Dudley Moore), sober for perhaps the first time in the film, is trying to feed his lifelong friend. They talk about food and they talk about dying and they talk about the woman Arthur is really in love with. They talk about everything but the point of the scene, which is how much they love each other, until the very end of the scene when Hobson says, "Arthur. You're a very good son." It is an extraordinary moment because it feels so out of left field. The stuffy Hobson's off-the-cuff admission that he'd always viewed Arthur as a surrogate son is incredibly moving.

There are instances in which endless speeches have worked — see Paddy Chayefsky's *Network* for the best example I know. But in general, part of the point here is to keep your characters' speeches short and crisp.

Sometimes context can make it possible to just come out and say what you mean. In *Amadeus*, Peter Schaffer used Old Salieri's battle to destroy the priest's faith as an excuse to talk directly about the theme of the movie as well as to describe the Young Salieri's motivation.

3. **Have you found a single line or phrase or exchange that basically sums up your film?** *Dirty Harry*'s "Do you feel lucky, punk?" *The Terminator*'s "I'll be back." *The Fugitive*'s "I didn't kill my wife!"/"I don't care!" As with the log line, the ability to boil your screenplay to a single Haiku-like moment indicates that you have a firm handle on your film's central idea.

4. **Read your script aloud** or, better yet, get others to read it to you. Does the dialogue feel natural? Do different characters

have different voices, or do they all sound the same? Is there excessive dialogue, or does it all feel necessary? Are you having characters repeat themselves?

Description and Action

Different writers develop different ways of dealing with writing description and action. Some talk directly to the reader. One well-paid screenwriter describes every single emotional beat an actor might go through in a scene, ending each line of description with an ellipsis instead of a period to ensure that the reader knows how much more he could have said. My own experience is that this kind of self-conscious writing works against you more often than it works for you. Clarity and brevity with the occasional flourish works best, in my opinion.

The main things are to provide a sense of forward motion and to establish a singular voice and consistent rhythm while keeping in mind that the screenplay is not a literary form. You are taking the reader by the seat of his or her pants and guiding him/her through your story. You are writing for people with a lot on their minds and little time. You want the journey through the script to be engaging and easy. You don't want your reader to feel lost because there are too many characters introduced at once, or because the geography or chronology are hard to follow. You want to bundle single ideas together, break paragraphs at new actions. You can use phrases instead of sentences to keep things moving.

Character description: When I was looking for examples of great character description to reference I picked up a collection of screenplays by William Goldman[5] and opened to the middle of *Marathon Man.* I could not put it down. Ditto for when I flipped to *Butch Cassidy and the Sundance Kid.* Goldman does some stuff that I do not recommend — namely, there is a "CUT TO" after each paragraph. But in all other respects he is the master and well worth studying.

---

5 Goldman, William. *Four Screenplays with Essays — Marathon Man, Butch Cassidy and the Sundance Kid, The Princess Bride, Misery.* Applause Books, New York, 1995.

Goldman established a very specific tone in his screenplay for *Butch Cassidy and the Sundance Kid* through a note that opens the script: "Not that it matters, but most of what follows is true." There is a kind of casualness implied, as though the whole thing is slightly out of focus. We are peering into the past and we're dealing with legends and we're just not going to get everything right. But it won't matter, because the story is going to be that good. How ballsy was Goldman to write that?

Here is Butch's introduction:

```
A man idly walking around the building. He is
BUTCH CASSIDY and hard to pin down. Thirty-
five and bright, he has brown hair, but most
people, if asked to describe him, would
remember him as blond. He speaks well and
quickly, and has been all his life a leader of
men, but if you asked him, he would be damned
if he could tell you why.
```

Look at what Goldman accomplished in Butch's intro to the reader. For one thing, he maintains the tone of the introductory sentence. Butch is "idly" casing a bank, a phrase that connotes casualness and comfort at what he is doing. He is described as thirty-five and "hard to pin down." What does that even mean? It means he's an interpreted character, an icon rather than a real person, and Goldman is giving us permission to make of him what we will. Ditto for the idea that he has brown hair but everyone sees him as blond. It means that this is a story about dinosaurs and this one is already fading from view.

We also learn that Butch is a leader but has no idea why, which means to me that he is modest but naturally charismatic. I get all that and yet the language continues to keep him at a distance, just slightly out of focus, in this case a way of connoting theme. And Goldman did not have to come out and say any of it.

Jeb Stuart shows a very different writing style in *The Fugitive*, but the entrance of Dr. Richard Kimble is also wonderfully efficient at telling a lot through the right details. In the original script we meet Kimble at the coat check for some benefit...

> The Man hands his coat to Coat Check Woman and thanks her. When he turns we get our first view of DR. RICHARD KIMBLE, a tall, athletic man, with a trim beard.
>
> He moves from the outer lobby into a fabulously decorated ballroom where a fashion show is taking place at a medical fundraiser. Doctors and their spouses, hospital brass and sponsors mingle. Women sit near the runway watching the models. Men talk by the bar. The room is packed.
>
> A banner over the rostrum says: "CHILDREN'S RESEARCH AND AID FOUNDATION"
>
> Kimble is handed a glass of champagne, which he promptly sets on another waiter's passing tray.

Things to note:

• Kimble thanks the Coat Check Girl. He is polite.

• The ballroom is "fabulously decorated" and there is a fashion show taking place. We definitely get the sense that Kimble is at the top of his game.

• Kimble takes a glass of champagne from one waiter but hands it off to the next one. Even at a party he is the responsible adult in the room.

Again, note how much information is given with the choice of the right details. Also note how taut and precise the writing is — there is not an extra word.

Action description: There are some general rules of thumb for writing compelling action — although there are (of course) spectacular examples that break these rules. But for the neophyte, here is a good starting place:

1. The object is to <u>propel</u> your reader through your script. Your language should be active and focused and, whenever possible, simple. You want your action descriptions to imply motion and energy. Sentences like "He starts to get up" do the opposite. It is, in fact, absurd — what does it mean to start to get up? Why not just say "He gets up?" Ditto for "She's standing." Nope. "She stands." Make your verbs active where possible.

2. Remember that readers tend to skim or even skip description, especially long paragraphs of it. Try to keep your descriptive paragraphs short, with short sentences or even fragments of sentences. The only time description is improved by length is when you are writing silent sequences, like the opening of Robert Towne's *Greystoke: The Legend of Tarzan*.

3. A single paragraph introducing a mass of characters can be a nightmare for a first-time reader. Ditto for complicated geography. In general, each paragraph should break for the next thought, or the next sequence of action.

4. Have you been as clear as possible about the choreography in your scenes, about the ages of your characters, about when you are in flashback and when you are in the present? Do not give your reader cause to feel lost.

5. Are you using inappropriate film-speak? Unless you know for certain that you are the director, elaborate directions for transitions and camera moves and music choices are a bad idea. Only use them when not doing so will obscure your intention for the story, or when (as in *Butch Cassidy and the Sundance Kid*) the camera is actually a character in the film.

6. Have you added scene numbers? Take them out. I know it may seem counter-intuitive, but the more professional you try to look the less professional you will come off. Since every experienced writer knows that the production team will put in their own numbers based on set-ups rather than the slug lines your screenwriting software identifies, including numbers tends to be viewed as amateurish.

Let's look at some examples. William Goldman's *Marathon Man* is a great place to start. As mentioned earlier, Goldman's style that drops a "CUT TO" between every paragraph is uniquely his and not something I suggest imitating. But take note of the intent, which is to draw the reader from scene to scene.

In *Marathon Man,* the character of Babe (Dustin Hoffman) gets caught up in the plot of aging Nazi Szell's plan to retrieve his diamonds from a bank vault. By the time we reach the following scene, Szell (Laurence Olivier) has murdered Babe's brother and tortured Babe for information Babe never had. Babe has escaped, Szell has retrieved his diamonds, and the following scene is part of their subsequent confrontation on the stairs of an apartment building. Szell has just opened his briefcase to show Babe the diamonds that fill it:

> CUT TO:

> SZELL, on his hands and knees, talking all the while as his right arm moves away from his body.

> SZELL
> You see? So many millions for us both —
> you must not pass up such a chance — I was
> right, do you understand?

> CUT TO:

> The FORTUNE and even in a blackout it would
> dazzle and — my God, how many millions of

dollars must there be in the briefcase, a
hundred, two hundred, more?

                                    CUT TO:

BABE, and there's really never ever been a
sight like it and transfixed, he kneels near
Szell by the diamonds and

                                    CUT TO:

SZELL, his right hand in motion, the knife
already sliding into killing position and as he
starts his swipe, a gunshot explodes and SZELL
staggers back a moment, and for a moment he
cannot believe what has happened as we

                                    CUT TO:

BABE, very calm, the gun in his hand, ready to
fire again. He's a very long way now from the
distraught kid we met early on.

SZELL'S disbelief gives way to something else:
he doesn't know what he's facing but it scares
him...

There is so much great stuff here it is hard to know where to start.
Notice first, I guess, how complete this is. We have jumped into the
middle of a scene and ended before the scene is over, but the sense of
suspense is so rooted in character that we can surmise enough about the
history between the two men to feel completely oriented in the moment.
Szell has a hidden knife and tries to lure Babe to his death. We get the
sense that the Babe he knew prior to this moment would have been an
easy mark, so Szell is completely certain of his own victory. But Babe
has changed, and Szell notices. Szell's reaction is all the more powerful
when you have read enough of the rest of the screenplay to know that
he is a notorious Nazi butcher who has never for a moment shown fear

of any individual, and that Babe is a mild-mannered student driven by circumstances to become a monster for this moment.

Goldman employs a number of techniques to involve us in this passage. The phrase "even in a blackout it would dazzle..." is compact enough that it doesn't slow down the read, but it gives a great sense of what Babe is looking at. Then Goldman lays in the "My God." For a moment he is talking to us, to the reader, and he's saying, "Holy crap, even I'm impressed." We almost feel like we are there with him looking at this fortune, so we are right there with Babe when he kneels down. Our fear that he has been seduced is increased because we have been seduced — even the writer has been seduced. Then the knife comes out — notice that Goldman points the camera at the knife but never at the gun until AFTER it is fired, so the shot is a surprise even though we know from earlier that he has the gun. That is key: the explosion is a reminder that the gun is there, not a new piece of information.

The tables are turned. Szell, who was completely calm while torturing Babe and gutting his brother, is now panicked, while Babe, who has spent a chunk of the film completely freaked out, is utterly calm in his new role as killer.

Notice how Goldman uses "and" in this passage to keep us in the thought. His sentences become like ticker tape, one long series of thoughts that draw us along. Not everyone can get away with this — it is a technique that has been overused — but the idea is right. Actually, short sentences and sentence fragments can accomplish the same thing. A more contemporary writer, trying not to be tagged as imitating Goldman might write Goldman's action as follows:

    SZELL slides his knife into killing position
    — starts his swipe. A gunshot explodes. SZELL
    staggers back, stunned.

It's interesting that Goldman just comes out and tells us that Babe is no longer the person we met at the beginning of the film. I think it works because it reinforces what we can see. It would not work if it was not self-evident.

Here is an action sequence from Jeb Stuart and David Twohy's script for *The Fugitive*. The technique is very different from Goldman's but it is still very effective.

This is the scene that immediately precedes the train hurtling into the bus in which Richard Kimble was being transported as a prisoner. Kimble, another prisoner named Coleman and two guards are alive on the bus, which is on its side. The Young Guard has been shot and Kimble has been trying to patch him up when he feels a shiver run through the bus:

```
EXT. RAILROAD TRACKS — NIGHT

The bus lays across railroad tracks. A not-too-
distant bend grows bright by the light of an
approaching train.

INT. BUS — NIGHT

Kimble sees: Old Guard fights the cage door.
Kimble lunges to his side.

                    KIMBLE
    It's locked. Where're your keys?

EXT. RAILROAD TRACKS — NIGHT

Down track, one Cyclops light appears.

INT. BUS — NIGHT

Kimble spots keys. Pitches them to Old Guard.
Drags Young Guard to the front for a quick
exit. But Old Guard fumbles the key-ring, his
hands shaking as much as the bus.

The train light spider-webs across cracked
windows. Kimble snatches the keys away from the
Guard's trembling hands.
```

KIMBLE
Which one? This? This one?!

Old Guard gulps a nod. Kimble jams a key in the
lock. Throws the door open. Grabs Young Guard.

KIMBLE
Help me get him -

But Old Guard climbs right over Kimble's back
and climbs out the shattered windshield.

Notice first that these writers do not insert camera or editorial directions. Not only that, there is a slug line introducing each shot. Many writers worry that doing this interrupts the flow of their action writing but that doesn't appear to be an issue here. Another technique is to drop the INT/EXT and the time (since the action is all continuous) and simply write...

FREIGHT TRAIN: As the WHEELS BRAKE and LOCK.

RAILROAD TRACKS: Kimble struggles out of the
bus — pulling the Young Guard behind.

Etc.

I quite like this modified version of action writing, but the truth is that either way works. The main point is, you have to indicate each new set-up — each new spot where you need to set a camera in order to see the action being described.

Other things to notice in this passage:

• The action keeps returning to the approaching train to build suspense.

• Note that no paragraph is longer than three lines. One action beat per paragraph.

• Just like Goldman used "My God" to such great effect, these writers dropped in, "Down track, one Cyclops light appears." The choice of the word "Cyclops" transforms the train into a monster bearing down on the bus. It changes the whole tone of the passage.

• Kimble is new at being a prisoner — his transformation from respected doctor to accused killer has been a violent one — but he is the calm one in the scene. The old guard, who was something of a bully when he had the gun and the prisoners were locked up, is now quaking too badly to even hang onto the keys.

• The Old Guard's cowardice is on full display when Kimble gets the window open and the Old Guard abandons his buddy and climbs right over Kimble to escape. Kimble is left to rescue the Young Guard.

Scenes

Are your scenes each mini-movies? Do they have clear beginnings, middles, and ends? Do you get in as late as possible and out as soon as possible? Is there a clear source of dramatic tension? A scene with no drama is not really a scene. If there is something important you feel needs to be said, it can't just show up in a scene of someone talking. There needs to be a dramatic context for the information.

Another question, harder to articulate, concerns subtext. Your characters do not always need to be talking about what the scene is about. Often it is much more elegant to do the opposite. A terrific example is the scene in *Howards End*, adapted from the E.M. Forster novel by Ruth Prawer Jhabvala, in which Helen (Helena Bonham Carter) opens her door to a rain-drenched Leonard (Samuel West) come to retrieve the umbrella he claims she has accidentally misappropriated. Helen chatters endlessly about which umbrella in her collection might be his, invites him to tea, tries to sweep him up in her nervous chatter about scones and how drenched he is. All the while, all he wants is to get a word in edgewise. But, though neither is able to articulate this, the scene is about his desperate longing for her and her utter inability to respond. (You can watch the scene at *http://www.tcm.com/mediaroom/video/449228/Howards-End-Movie-Clip-You-Took-My-Umbrella.html.*)

Length

One of the things that invariably happens in rewrite is that your script will grow in length. The notes people give you always seem to want you to add things, clarify things. Although in reality clarity often involves the "less is more" principle, no one seems to give that note. So suddenly you find yourself staring at a 140-page opus. This can be a big issue that must be addressed as part of the polish process.

Submitting an over-long screenplay can be a disaster. Your readers' hearts will sink if it is too long because (a) they know it will take longer to get through; and (b) an over-long script is more often than not a script in need a lot of work. You can deliver a 130-page historical drama. A 130-page romantic comedy will make you a candidate for the let's-never-read-them-again list.

As mentioned earlier, one of the reasons for the uniformity of Warner script format is so that executives, producers, and directors will know exactly how long your screenplay is. It was developed by the fabulous Script Processing Department at Warner Bros. Every draft of a project in development there is put into strict Warner format so the execs can track how long the film will run — and whether or not writers are obeying the edict to cut pages. I have worked with more than one writer who tried to "cut" by changing the margins.

With any luck your script will get made and when it does there will probably be a contractual running time to be met. So if you have somehow managed to sneak an over-long script past your producers and executives, then you are guaranteed that some of it will be left on the cutting room floor, often to disastrous results. I'll give you an example: I worked once with a writer-director who would not eliminate certain sequences that both made the film too long and added an unnecessary twist to the plot. So the script was shot as written. When the cut came in too long we brought in one of Hollywood's premier editorial doctors to help us. His first move was to try ditching those exact sequences.

Unfortunately, we hadn't shot a script that supported those cuts, so we were forced to lose other stuff that would have enriched the film. This was a double-loss: Not only did the film lose some emotional resonance, but also we'd wasted badly needed production dollars on scenes we never should have shot.

The truth is, all of us who have been reading for years can spot a cheat anyway. Most screenwriting programs have a tab that allows you to format your script in Warner format. You might as well use it.

How do you go about losing pages? Every script is different, of course, and so presents different challenges. But there are some guidelines:

- The only scenes in your movie should be scenes that move the story forward and illuminate character. The exception is in a comedy, when you are allowed scenes that are only there to be funny. So go through and weed out anything that feels superfluous. If the story would work without the scene, lose it.

- Long paragraphs of description do you no good at all. Trim them back to the bare minimum. Phrases are often better than sentences. I know a writer who took a whole paragraph of description of the shape of the mountains and the movement of the fog and the sense of foreboding it presented and reduced all of it to, "EXT. MISTY MOUNTAINTOP — DUSK."

- Make sure that you are getting into your scenes as late as possible and exiting as soon as possible. As a great example, look at how Robert Towne's *Chinatown* opens. We come into the first scene in private eye Jake Gittes' office after he has shown his client Curly photos proving that Curly's wife cheated on him. Towne knew he didn't need to show Jake open a drawer and take out the photos and hand them to Curly, nor did he need to show Curly's build to despair. So he discarded all that and brought us in on Curly's reaction, which told us everything we needed to know.

- "Shoe-leather" is usually trim-able. Do we really need to see every entrance and exit? Every walk to the kitchen? As with nearly everything else in this book, there are fantastic exceptions to this rule. *Run Lola Run* is entirely about shoe leather.

• Exposition: If you have long speeches of exposition, chances are you need to find a more efficient — and probably a more visual — way of delivering the information. How much of the exposition is really necessary? How much is necessary now? How much can we infer from the visuals? From other characters' dialogue? A missing tooth can speak to a character's hard life or down-on-his-luck circumstances better than a sentence of description.

Title

Titles are tough. I grew up knowing a guy who paid for his swimming pool thinking of titles for films. You are looking for something that describes and sells your film, that captures the energy of the piece, and that feels like it is a hook.

Films rarely have titles longer than three words. (This excludes titles with subtitles, like the Harry Potter films.) *Three Men and a Baby* worked, as did *Eternal Sunshine of the Spotless Mind*. But in general, short is good. Dynamic is good. *Independence Day* when combined with the trailer and poster images was genius. *Titanic* and *Avatar* and *Transformers* all named the subject of the film. *Days of Thunder* was evocative. *Butch Cassidy and the Sundance Kid* is maybe the exception that proves the rule. I suppose they could have called it *Butch and Sundance*, sort of like *Bonnie and Clyde*. But in this case whole names probably were more musical.

Proofreading — The final step of the polish

This final point should go without saying and yet it is shocking how often it is an issue: **Do not ever submit a screenplay until you have proofed it and then proofed it again and then had a friend proof it.** I can tell you the reason from the first-hand experience of hurling scripts across my yard. There was a long period when I was bringing home as many as eighteen scripts to read each weekend. That was enough to restrict my weekend recreation to carrying the pile of submissions from my desk to a lounge chair in the garden. If in the stack that was claiming so much of my time I came across a script written by someone who couldn't be bothered to correct typos and misspellings and formatting issues, it would enrage me all out of proportion to the offense. I found it unbearably rude. I would not finish the script. And I was not alone in this reaction.

Proofing is the easiest thing to do and the most inexcusable to blow off. I suppose, actually, that this should have been the first rule of the screenwriting process: **Do not enrage the people who can get your scripts made.**

EXERCISES

Polishing your screenplay

Read through your screenplay (yes, again), looking at the following:

1. Working with the first ten pages of your rewritten draft, strip out all of the dialogue.
   a. How readable are those pages? Note where you get lost or confused and make the fixes so that no one paragraph tries to communicate too many ideas and so that you feel you are being drawn through the scenes.
   b. In paragraphs of action:
      i. If the paragraph is longer than three sentences, look to see if there is a way to trim it or break it up.
      ii. Is the movement of the action clear?
      iii. Have you used active verbs?
      iv. Have you used exactly the right words to convey the energy and mood of the action? Is the action easy to follow?
      v. Does each paragraph propel you to the next?
      vi. Is the action a reflection of character? Of theme?

    c. In paragraphs of description:

        i. In paragraphs of description that are longer than three sentences, are there ways to trim?

        ii. Have you chosen to include only the most relevant and evocative details? Are there details you could drop? Do the details you have included paint a clear picture? Are they the details most relevant to the story you are telling?

        iii. Do your descriptions of characters contain information about who that character is as well as how he/she looks? Is their dress, manner of movement — their physical appearance in general — evocative of who they are?

2. Add back the dialogue. There is no easy way to do this. I would maybe activate "track changes" when you are working on the dialogue-free pages and then go back and lay those changes in to the original pages.

    a. Is each character's dialogue a reflection of who he or she is?

    b. In speeches longer than three lines, are their lines to trim?

    c. Is your dialogue too on-the-nose? Are you making good use of subtext?

    d. In speeches that communicate exposition, is that exposition presented in a dramatic context? Is it necessary? Are you presenting at a moment when it will be most useful? Are there ways to present it other than verbal?

    e. Read your dialogue out loud. Does it roll easily off the tongue? Does it feel natural?

3. Do this for your entire screenplay.

9 A CLOSER LOOK:
Little Miss Sunshine, The King's Speech, Lincoln

The ensemble film: *Little Miss Sunshine*

I have been writing entirely about films with single protagonists. This is because ensemble pieces very rarely get the green light. Distributor marketing departments like to have a single star on which to hang the campaign. But ensemble films can get made, and they can be brilliant.

The answer to the question of how one structures an ensemble film is both simple and complicated. Simple in that it is mostly a matter of emphasis: There is almost always a main story that the other stories wrap around. Each main character is the star of his or her own complete film, and all of the same rules apply but in multiples. The big difference is that each of those "films" has close to the same weight in the final product. What makes it complicated is the way these subplots need to interact with one another, each energizing the main story at key points. Writing an ensemble piece is akin to playing a good game of billiards. The writer needs to know the physics of how the different balls of story will career off one another.

The screenplay I want to study for this discussion (I am working from the original script, not from the final film) is called *Little Miss Sunshine* — which in most films would be an indication of who the protagonist is. This is both true and not true here. The pretext for the plot is the journey a dysfunctional family takes to get Olive, the youngest member, to a "Little Miss Sunshine" beauty contest in Florida. It is her "want" that motivates the grand action of the film. But as we'll see, this only nominally makes her the film's protagonist. Everyone has their own agenda on this journey, and the story is really about the collision of these agendas and the impact that each character has upon the others. Olive has the smallest arc, and she is relatively passive through most of the film, jumping in only when necessary.

This is a true ensemble film in which all of the main characters and their very complete subplots have equal weight. At the end of the day it feels like the family itself, with all of its different personalities, is the protagonist — a living, complex organism that wants to get Olive to the beauty competition but needs more than anything and against all odds to survive as a family.

Michael Arndt delivered a magnificent screenplay. The character work is sublime, the theme — that winners are defined only by their passion and willingness to be in the game — is stated and re-stated in the most dramatic contexts. The film benefitted enormously from a spectacular cast (Abigail Breslin, Greg Kinnear, Alan Arkin, Toni Collette, Paul Dano, and Steve Carell) and pitch-perfect direction by Jonathan Dayton and Valerie Faris, but it all originated in the mind of screenwriter Arndt. So it seems well worth dissecting to see how it all works.

Life before the plot kicks in:
- Olive: The script opens on a televised beauty contest. Six-year-old Olive watches it, entranced. She practices waving like the winning Miss Florida, a poignant moment because Olive is a pudgy little girl with a body not built for beauty contests. This is her character contradiction and it defines her right from the opening frames of the film.

- Richard: We next meet Olive's stepfather Richard (45), teaching the last class of the semester at a community college. The lecture is about his theory that winners and losers choose their own fate. The implication is that there is no worse label than "loser." The few people in the classroom don't seem to care much, a fact that Richard ignores. His oft-repeated edicts on what makes a winner and what makes a loser is the first statement of the thematic issue of the film. Also, please note Richard's character contradiction: He preaches about how to be a winner but seems to be trapped in a life in which even he views himself as a loser.

- Sheryl and Frank: Sheryl (40s), Olive's mother, wears a blazer and a name tag, details that tell us she is in a low-paying and low-excitement job. She is at the hospital to pick up her brother Frank who has just survived a suicide attempt. The hospital can't keep him because he has no insurance, another detail about the family's financial situation. On the phone with Richard, Sheryl denies she is smoking while puffing away, an indication of the state of her marriage. Sheryl tells Frank, "I'm so glad you're still here." To which he responds, "Well, that makes one of us." The line sets up both his state of mind and his sarcastic voice.

- Grandpa: When we meet Grandpa (80s) he is snorting heroin. We learn a bit later that he is also Olive's private coach for her beauty pageant dance routine.

- Dwayne: Dwayne is Olive's 15-year-old brother. Dwayne has a Mohawk haircut, a poster of Nietzsche in his room, and a calendar on which he marks off the days left until he can enlist in the Navy. He does not speak a word until much later in the film.

Note that we pick up these characters fairly late in their stories. Frank has already attempted suicide, Olive has committed herself to entering a beauty contest and is rehearsing a routine with her grandfather, Dwayne has committed himself to his dream of flying for the Navy, Richard and Sheryl are already aware they are going nowhere fast. Each is trapped in some way, knows they are trapped, and yearns to break free. And Richard's constant harangue about winners and losers is an intolerable reminder to all of them that their intolerable lives are their own fault, and that the world will judge them as losers.

Also, let's look at the **names** Michael Arndt chose. Frank, Sheryl and Richard are all sort of average names for average people. Olive feels a bit more exotic, like her parents had dreams for her. Dwayne actually feels guy-ish and military, but also slightly old-fashioned. And Grandpa isn't named until he dies, a perfect reflection of the way he feels — invisible and irrelevant.

The next sequence is at Sheryl and Richard's home. Because Frank can't be left alone, Sheryl has set up a cot for him in Dwayne's room. Neither Dwayne nor Frank is happy about the arrangement, especially when Frank sees that his cot has a Cookie Monster sleeping bag. He is a grown man and (we will learn) the nation's preeminent Proust scholar — and his life has been reduced to that of a toddler. This is the **inciting incident** in the Frank/Dwayne relationship story.

Richard returns home and barely acknowledges his family as he races to the answering machine, which tells us that whatever he is waiting for is the most important thing in his life — he is desperate for a change. We learn he is waiting for a call from his agent Stan Grossman who has promised to sell his book about his Nine-Step Program. Unfortunately, the only message is from Olive's father Jeff reporting that the winner of the Little Miss Sunshine beauty contest was disqualified and so Olive is now the winner — which means she is eligible for the state contest in Florida. This news would be the first plot point except that everyone is too stressed to really pay any attention. This sets up some anticipation about whether or not Olive will miss her opportunity.

Richard snaps at Sheryl when she asks what is going on with Stan, another indication of how close to the breaking point Richard, Sheryl and their marriage are. This lack of expected news is the **inciting incident** in the story about their relationship, and in particular in Richard's story. Richard needs an answer from Grossman and spends considerable energy during the rest of the script trying to get one.

In Dwayne's bedroom, Frank sits staring at a photo from his wallet so we know his suicide attempt was probably over the loss of someone. Silent Dwayne signs that dinner is ready and we learn that he stopped speaking because of Nietzsche. "Far out," says Uncle Frank. So we know that Dwayne is an interesting kid and that Frank might turn out to be the only adult who understands him. The potential for a bond between them is strengthened when they are left alone at the dinner table. Dwayne writes on a tablet that he hates everyone. When Frank asks if that includes him Dwayne writes, "Not yet." "Fair enough," says Frank. The challenge is on: Dwayne's loathing is not universal, it is specific and he hasn't made up his mind about Frank.

Sheryl explains that Dwayne has taken a vow of silence until he can join the Naval Academy as a pilot. Olive and Grandpa finally come up from rehearsing her routine in the basement and we learn that no one has seen it yet — this sets the stage for the film's **big secret**. Innocent Olive goes straight to Frank and kisses him, then asks about the bandages on his wrist. Grandpa gets angry about having to eat KFC again and we learn he was kicked out of his retirement home for doing heroin.

When Frank asks how long Dwayne has been silent he is told it has been nine months. Richard jumps in to announce that he has decided he's really proud of Dwayne for going for his dream just like Richard's Nine-Step Program prescribes. No one wants to hear it.

Olive asks again what happened to Frank. Richard says Frank was sick and wants to leave it at that, but Frank bulls through and explains that he was in love with a male grad student who left him for a guy named Gary Sugarman, the nation's number-two Proust scholar. Of being in love with a guy Olive says, "That's silly." But that's not the end of Frank's story. After he lost his lover he lost his job and his apartment — and then learned that Gary won a MacArthur genius grant for his writing on Proust. Of his suicide attempt he says, "I failed at that as well." Note that the only **backstories** we learn in any detail are Frank's and Grandpa's.

Richard's response to Frank is to explain to Olive, "Frank gave up on himself, which is something winners never do." Frank asks Dwayne,

"Is he always like this?" and Dwayne nods, "Yes." When Frank asks how he can stand it, Dwayne writes, "I can't." Their bond is complete.

Note that we are nearing the end of Act One, and we know the character contradictions that will power this film:

- Olive wants to be a beauty queen but has a body and an innocence that makes her success pretty unlikely.

- Richard preaches about how winners are people who choose to be winners but he is in fact in a loser job trying to teach bored community college students an obviously loser philosophy.

- Frank is passionate about a subject no one cares about and in love with a man who loves someone else. He feels like a complete loser — he even failed at suicide — and wants to end his life but has too much respect for his sister's family to do it on their watch. This makes him a completely dispassionate observer — and, by the way, allows him to say some stuff we'd like to say to some of these characters.

- Grandpa is old and yearns for escape but underneath his frustration he genuinely loves his family. He is also the most colorful character but the only one who Arndt doesn't name.

- Dwayne is young and yearns for escape from his totally dysfunctional family, but his planned path turns out to be completely impossible. (We learn the second half of this later.)

- Sheryl is trying her best to hold it all together, but she is strapped for cash, working in a dead end job, and is the only responsible adult in a family that includes a six-year-old with an impossible dream, a rebellious teenager, a lost husband, a heroin-snorting father-in-law, and a suicidal brother.

We know everyone's contradiction and have a sense of the journey on which the film will take them.

So far, all of these have been separate stories, only linked by proximity. We are right before the first plot point that changes everyone's life and so it is worth pausing to see what has happened structurally. As mentioned earlier, in some ways (though this would be a really unconventional view) the protagonist of the film is this totally dysfunctional family that wants to survive. Each member's story has its own inciting incident:

- Olive's happened off camera, before the film started, when she won runner-up in the Little Miss Sunshine contest, because that is what gave her hope.

- Grandpa's also happened off camera when he got tossed from the old age home where he got to be the house stud. Moving in with his son and family has robbed him of freedom, women, and dignity. The only useful thing he does is train Olive.

- For the rest of them, Frank's arrival at his sister's house is the inciting incident.
  - Frank's normal life was unbearable, but now it has just gotten unimaginably worse.
  - Ditto for Dwayne — Frank's arrival has made it impossible to maintain the solitude he craves.
  - Richard's teaching gig has ended, he is strapped for cash, all of his focus is on selling his book — and now Frank is there as a proud example of a loser and the only person willing to stand up to him. To Richard's eye, Frank is everything he hates.
  - Frank's arrival has pushed Sheryl's burden over the top. It is more responsibility than she can bear.

And now... Olive finally replays Jeff's message and is ecstatic, racing around the house to pack for the trip to Florida she assumes is in the cards. This is the **first plot point** for all of them, offering everyone the chance for a road trip. Not everyone is thrilled at first because it means they will all be trapped together. But Olive's father Jeff has planned to leave town and so is immediately eliminated as a transportation option, and it turns out Sheryl promised Olive she'd take her. Sheryl wants to just fly down but Richard says they can't really afford that. The simmering feud between them surfaces briefly when Sheryl says they'd be able to pay for the trip if she had any help, but Richard reassures her that all will be fine once they hear from Stan. This sets up one of the **ticking clocks** — we know that in Richard's story everything depends on that conversation with Stan. A second and more inclusive clock is set because they have a limited amount of time to get to Florida.

Frank doesn't want to go but there is no way Sheryl can leave him alone. Dwayne doesn't want to go, but Sheryl bribes him by saying she'll sign the permission slip for him to join the Naval Academy. So they all pile into the family VW van.

The van is a new and fantastically important character in the film. It is like some cherub sent by God to push them all to the breaking point. It is not the antagonist *per se* because it does not appear in the film's finale. But it is a close runner up.

So now we are at the start of Act Two. The overall goal is to get Olive to the competition on time. But whereas Olive is ecstatic, everyone else has an added layer — they want the least amount of stress possible. Frank and Dwayne sum it up when Dwayne says he'll go, "But I'm not going to have any fun." Frank responds, "We're all with you on that, Dwayne."

Before we get into Act Two, I want to pause and discuss the **antagonist**. In some ways, Richard is everyone's antagonist — his *sub rosa* rage and constant lecturing make everyone feel like crap. Even though he is driving everyone toward the competition, his attitude is toxic. He eventually sabotages Olive's confidence and so weakens her chances of reaching her goal. Her performance in the end is as much about winning his appreciation and approval as anything. Richard has become the personification of the world that wants to judge people on some arbitrary, surfacey basis and not love them for who they are.

As we'll see, this demon called judgment inhabits various people throughout the film — Frank in the form of self-loathing, Dwayne who loathes and judges his own family, other beauty pageant competitors and their parents who judge Olive's entry as ridiculous, and the judges themselves. It is Olive's fearless willingness to take this demon on that ultimately redeems everyone we care about. Does this make Olive the hero of the film? Well, on one level the answer is yes. But on another level everyone in the film behaves in a heroic way in battling their demons, which is what makes it a true ensemble movie.

I might also argue that the VW van is Richard's antagonist, making it increasingly difficult for him to deliver the family on time to the competition. Its breakdowns are perfectly timed to bring him to his lowest point in the film.

Act Two: Richard forces Olive to state that she's sure she'll win the contest before he allows everyone to pile into the van, their first step toward the goal of reaching the competition on time. Olive has her headphones on so Grandpa feels free to offer Dwayne some sage advice: "Fuck a lot of women." He admits that he got tossed from the home for doing smack. "Now I'm stuck with Mr. Happy here," he says, defining his attitude and his relationship with his son. But his obsession with women and his raunchy attitude is another clue leading to the reveal of the big secret — and it turns out in the end that his who-cares-what-anyone-else-thinks attitude has a lot to do with Olive winning the day.

The next sequence is in a diner. When Olive apologizes to the waitress for not having made her decision, Richard tells her not to apologize. "It's a sign of weakness." This is a great set-up for a moment later in the act.

Richard tries to make Olive feel bad about ordering ice cream — someone who really wants to win the beauty competition wouldn't eat something that could make them fat. Frank leads the charge trying to diffuse the situation and Olive has her ice cream, but Richard has left his mark on her. This is sort of a midpoint in Olive's story, a turning point in her attitude toward herself.

Sheryl announces she wants to learn to drive a stick shift — she is mad enough at Richard's ice cream remarks to say, "If you can do it, how hard can it be?" But it turns out the van's clutch is broken.

Dwayne gets really pissy while they all await the mechanic's prognosis. Frank, who is sort of done with everyone's intolerance for each other, explains to Dwayne that when he was growing up Sheryl was the cool one. "What happened?" Dwayne writes. Frank responds, "She had you, Dwayne." Dwayne is smart enough to be rocked by this thought. A great, quiet stop-judging-people moment.

It is worth pausing again to note how each subplot is connected by this theme of judgment. Frank breaks through to Dwayne by pointing out why his judgment of his mother might be off base. Frank was suicidal because his lover's boyfriend got judged to be a genius and not him. Richard is a mess because no one but him thinks his paradigm for making winners and losers is worth anything. Olive is headed to Florida to be judged. All of these different stories fit together because of their thematic link.

The auto mechanic explains that the van's clutch is shot and can't be fixed in time to get the family to Florida. They are all ready to give up but the mechanic insists that they don't need the clutch as long as they are willing to push the van to start it and only drive in third and fourth gears. As they all gather at the rear of the van to push, Frank reminds them all that he is the nation's foremost scholar of Marcel Proust. It is a funny moment, but it is also a clever way of keeping the thought in our minds, which will be important in a bit.

They get the van started and nearly leave Frank behind but Dwayne helps him catch up and everyone cheers him. It is the first smile we get from Dwayne. It is also another step in the bromance between Frank and Dwayne.

The next leg of the trip is marked by boredom. We learn an important fact, though: Richard's agent Stan is at an expo in Atlanta trying to sell the book. When Richard tries to explain his ideas to Frank, they get into an argument. Sheryl tries to break it up and Frank says petulantly, "It's his fault." Everyone laughs except for Richard, who is wound too tight at this point. Richard is rapidly approaching his low point.

The tension is broken when Richard's phone rings. He has no reception, however, so they pull over at a gas station to use the payphone. While Richard calls Stan, Frank offers to get everyone drinks. Grandpa quietly asks him to buy some good porno. Frank shrugs and heads inside — where he runs into his former lover. The reunion is very awkward as Frank tries to hide his bandaged wrists and pretend that life is great. When he later peers out the window he sees his ex-lover climb into Gary Sugarman's Jaguar and laugh, probably at his expense. A big step toward his low point.

Richard storms back to the van and will only say that the deal didn't work out. Sheryl is furious. "You said it was a done deal," she yells as they drive off. Their argument is cut short when Frank notices that they left Olive behind. They go back for her. A great — and very funny — beat indicating that the whole family is forgetting the important things.

Grandpa, visibly worried about his son, climbs to the front of the van and tells Richard he's proud of him, saying that very few people try something on their own. Grandpa forces a sullen Richard to acknowledge what he said. We see that underneath Grandpa's boiling rage is a caring father that Richard refuses to acknowledge.

At a motel for a night, Olive bunks with Grandpa. Dwayne and Frank share a room from which they can hear Richard and Sheryl yell at each other about their financial future. Richard says, "I trusted him, okay? Step Three is you have to trust people!" And Sheryl shoots back, "Fuck the Nine Steps, Richard! They're not working! It's over!! Forget it!! I never want to hear the Nine Steps again!!" The line makes Dwayne smile.

Back in Grandpa's room, Olive confesses that she is scared of being a loser. "Dad hates losers," she says. Grandpa states the real point of the film: "Whoa, whoa, back up a second. You can't lose. You know why? Because a real loser isn't someone who doesn't win. A real loser is someone who's so afraid of <u>not</u> winning they don't even try." He tucks her in, then retreats to the bathroom to snort heroin. The contradiction provides great irony: Grandpa feels old and judged for who he is and so has essentially given up. Does that make him a loser? Well, no. In the context of this film it makes him fierce — he is definitely not going gentle into that good night.

Sheryl tells Richard she's considering a trial separation. Richard says, "I'm going to fix this," and slams out of the room. This is the midpoint in the Richard/Sheryl story.

Unable to get the van started, Richard rents some local kid's moped and drives to Atlanta to confront Stan about why he hasn't been able to sell the program. Stan fires back, "It's not the program. It's you. No one's heard of you. Nobody cares." Richard tries to salvage some dignity by firing Stan for giving up, but the script tells us this is the lowest moment of his life. Or that's what he thinks until it starts pouring rain while he's riding the moped back to the motel. This is a great tease — it really does look like things could not get any worse for Richard. But as I said earlier, part of good screenwriting is sadism, and Michael Arndt is not finished with Richard yet.

Back in the motel room there is a sweet moment when Richard climbs into bed and Sheryl asks if he's okay. But then things actually do get worse when Olive shows up with the news that grandpa won't wake up.

In the hospital waiting room, Sheryl tells her kids the truth of their financial situation but insists all will be okay because, "We're a family." When she cries, Dwayne writes on his pad for Olive to go hug her, but he won't go to her himself. He cares but can't let himself show it.

It turns out that grandpa is dead and there is so much red tape to deal with that there is no way for them to reach the competition in time. Structurally this is an interesting moment. Notice how the stories wrap around one another. This is really the **low point** for the character of Richard — he has just lost his dream project, he's broke, his dad is dead and he can't even get his daughter to her beauty competition. It is also the **midpoint** of Olive's journey, though she is at this point a passive player.

At this point Richard's story takes over for a moment when he decides he is not going to be defeated by his foolish father. The entire family colludes in stealing the body and loading it into the van's trunk and off they go.

Once on the road again we get an incredibly sweet moment of Olive asking if her grandfather is in heaven. We know he was a smack-addicted porno freak, but he was Olive's rock and in her innocence that's all she knows. And, putting all judgment aside, that's really what he was.

They drive in silence for a bit. Sheryl keeps glancing at her husband, even rubs his neck — there is compassion there even through her fear for the future. Dwayne is stoic as usual. But they are late and the van is still conspiring against them: When someone cuts them off Richard honks and the horn gets stuck. So of course they get stopped by a cop.

Richard apologizes for the horn and Frank ribs him, "Don't apologize. It's a sign of weakness." Shaken, Richard keeps glancing at the trunk, causing the cop to want it opened. Knowing he is doomed, Richard obliges — but Grandpa's porno tumbles out and the happy cop confiscates it and leaves, never even noticing the corpse. Grandpa's porno addiction proves at that moment to have been a good thing. No point judging him for it. Note again that pretty much every detail is in service of the film's theme.

Later than ever, Frank makes the discovery that Dwayne is colorblind. This is tragic news — Frank says it means Dwayne will not be accepted into the Navy. Dwayne freaks out. Richard pulls over and Dwayne bolts, collapsing into a field and screaming his first word of the film: "Fuck!!!!!"

Sheryl tries to comfort her son with words about the importance of family but Dwayne screams, "You're not my family! I don't want to be your family! I hate you! (points at each of them) Divorce! Bankrupt! Suicide! You're losers! You're fucking losers!"

No one knows what to do. This of course is the **low point** in Dwayne's story but also of the family's — It looks, finally, like they have been defeated in their play to get Olive to the hotel in time. But then Olive goes to Dwayne and silently puts her arm around him. Dwayne has a decision to make, and his love for Olive wins out. He says, "Okay, let's go," apologizes for all he just said and they are off on the final leg of the trip. This was the **second plot point that spins us into Act Three.**

Richard can't find the entrance to the hotel conference center, drives over the divide to get there, they rush inside — and are four minutes late. The nasty official won't bend the rules for them, claiming that they have shut down all their computers, but when Richard throws himself on his knees to beg, the sound guy offers to enter them into the system.

Other Barbie-like contestants make fun of Olive, but she only has eyes for the Miss Florida she saw win in the film's opening. Olive stands in line to meet her. All she wants to know is if Miss Florida eats ice cream, and is ecstatic to learn she does. We can see that the idea that others judge her differently than she judges herself is starting to percolate into her brain.

Frank and Dwayne get a room, where Frank opens *The New York Times* to discover an ad for his nemesis Gary Sugarman's "surprise best seller" about Proust. Frank briefly considers suicide but decides against it. Clearly, this is his **low point** in the film. Note how each of these subplots leapfrog one another to keep the tension up.

Richard phones a local morgue and stands by while the medics cart off his father. Richard is left alone in the parking lot with only a small cardboard box of his father's things. Meanwhile, Frank and Dwayne head for the beach while Olive tries on her costume. Looking around at her competition, she approaches a mirror and sucks in her stomach for the first time, the result of as much from Richard's insidious talk at the diner as it from all of the implicit judgment surrounding her.

Richard gives Olive a "pep talk" that proves he still has not learned his lesson. Surrounded by living Barbies primping like poodles, he tells her that all the terrible stuff the family went through to get there will be worth it if she wins. Sheryl is disgusted with him.

Richard takes a seat in the house next to a biker/dad who wears ear plugs — and becomes increasingly nervous about Olive competing against these tiny, trained girl/women.

At the beach, Dwayne asks Frank what it felt like when he cut his wrists and Frank replies, "You know, I wish I could tell you I felt bad. But I didn't. I was outside the world, y'know? It was very peaceful. But

I'm feeling that way now, too, so..." Dwayne admits that he wishes he could just skip the painful high school years and Frank tells him about Proust. "Total loser. Never had a real job. Unrequited love affairs. Gay. Spent twenty years writing a book almost no one reads. But... he was also probably the greatest writer since Shakespeare. Anyway, he gets down to the end of his life, he looks back and he decides that all the years he suffered, those were the best years of his life. Because they made him who he was. They forced him to think and grow, and to feel very deeply. And the years he was happy? Total waste. Didn't learn anything."

Frank is rewarded with a grin from Dwayne. He continues, "So if you sleep 'til you're 18 think of all the suffering you'll miss! High school is your prime suffering years!" And Dwayne, on page 94 of a 110-page script, has his epiphany, a brilliantly dramatic excuse to re-state the **theme** of the film. "Fuck beauty contests," he says. "It's like life is one fucking beauty contest after another these days. School, then college, then work. Fuck it. Fuck the Naval Academy. Fuck the MacArthur Foundation. If I want to fly, I'll find a way to fly. You do what you have to and fuck the rest."

We are roaring into the **finale** now:

- On stage a tiny girl taps dances.

- Frank and Dwayne enter the venue wearing "Loser" t-shirts they just bought.

- Another tiny blonde does her cute show-tune routine.

- Backstage, skinny girls whine to their stage mothers.

- Richard corners Sheryl backstage and tells her he's decided he doesn't want Olive to go on. He knows how it feels to lose and he is certain she can't win. Sheryl is outraged — but then Dwayne shows up with the same sentiment — he doesn't want "those people" judging her. "You're the mom! You're supposed to protect her." Olive overhears her brother pronounce, "She's not a beauty queen, mom." Sheryl insists that it is Olive's choice and they have to back her...

The stage manager says it is time. Olive sits in the make-up chair and refuses to look at her mother. Sheryl says she doesn't have to go — and Olive gets up and marches onto the stage. She looks completely different than any of the other girls and the other kids make fun of her. But Olive dedicates her performance to her grandfather and signals her new best friend the sound guy, who starts Olive's loud, hard, and nasty music — different than anything else thus far.

Look at the gift Arndt gives his character through his description: "Olive turns and strides up the stage, hands on hips, shoulders swinging with an absolute and spectacular physical confidence... She dances with a total command — an exuberant, even witty mastery of her body, the music, the moves, everything. Most of all, she's doing it for herself — for her own sense of fun — and the judges are instantly irrelevant."

Of course, her grandfather being the porno hound that he was, the dance is also entirely inappropriate for that stage — this is the reveal of the film's **big secret**. The audience is stunned when she does a series of pelvic bumps. But Frank laughs and cheers. Richard cautiously joins, then Sheryl and Dwayne. The nasty official from the lobby tries to stop her — but Richard leaps onto the MC and yells, "Keep dancing, honey!" When the official demands that she leave the stage or be disqualified, Richard says, "Okay," and joins her dance. By the end the entire family is there with her, the sound guy has cranked up the music — and as a final beat Olive lifts her skirt to show she has written "peach" on her tummy. She gets a standing ovation.

We cut to all of them except Olive handcuffed together in some office. A cop agrees to free them only if they promise to never enter another beauty contest in Florida. No one has any problem promising that.

Outside, Sheryl puts a tiara on Richard's head. He removes it, puts it on Olive. She struggles to articulate something, finally shyly states, "I just like dancing." Everyone tells her how great she was and they head out. Olive's line is the great statement of the film: She was great because she was doing what she loved. And Grandpa was her ally, helping her as best he could without judging her in the least.

The last we see this family they are at a picnic table, relaxed and happy. The family organism, which wanted to get Olive to the contest, really needed to heal itself by coming together, and in that it has succeeded. Richard tells a funny story about his father and they toast to him. Richard's last line is, "Who wants some ice cream?"

Of the many things that make this script work so beautifully, the thing that impresses me the most is how these stories both leapfrog and bolster one another. Each segment of a subplot advances both that subplot and the script as a whole, bringing this initially dysfunctional family together by the time Olive does her dance. Nothing goes as planned so reverses abound. Each character has faced their demons and resolved their conflict so that they can be there as a family to support Olive, whose own contradiction turns out to be no conflict for her at all because she is so completely comfortable with who she is. Each of these subplots is compete, with its own beginning, middle, and end, but each ending — the collapse of Richard's dream, grandpa's death, Dwayne's discovery that he is colorblind — provides a new crisis that energizes the story. Frank is the only character whose crisis took place before the story of the film began, and his observations serve as Greek chorus for the audience and as catalyst for the family's recovery. It is a brilliantly structured screenplay that warrants a couple of close reads.

The King's Speech: **No, the flawed hero is not his own antagonist**

I have chosen to analyze this script, written by David Seidler, for one reason: to try to satisfy myself as to the identity of the antagonist. This is one of those films about which people keep insisting that the protagonist himself is his own worst enemy and therefore the antagonist of the film. I knew as I started to study this that that could not be the case, but I was not at all sure yet what the answer was. So this began as my own exploration into that question. As we shall see, it ended up being much more.

1925: We learn in a crawl that King George V reigns over a quarter of the world's population, setting the stage for the magnitude of the responsibility that looms over whoever ascends the throne in his wake.

At a BBC broadcasting house, King George asks his second son Bertie to approach the microphone and give the closing speech to The Empire Exhibition at Wembley, London. The BBC announcer who precedes Bertie speaks in "flawless pear-shaped tones" as he describes the importance and size of the crowd. Bertie gets encouragement from his wife Elizabeth — "truly an English rose" — and from Archbishop Cosmo Lang, but his walk down the corridor to meet the microphone in battle is more like a death march — and when it comes time he can't get the words out past his stutter. Rain disperses the disappointed crowd.

We are on page 4 of a 90-page screenplay. Seidler has given us Bertie's extraordinary **ordinary life** — He is second in line to take on the enormous responsibility that comes with being King. He is surrounded by sycophants, a lovely and loving wife, and an utterly insensitive father — and he is utterly unable to address a crowd because of a punishing stutter.

At Bertie's regal residence, a pompous medic counsels him to inhale deeply from a cigarette so the smoke can relax his lungs, then try to read through a mouth full of marbles. When Bertie explodes in frustration, the medic tells him this was the cure that worked for Demosthenes. Bertie replies, "That was ancient Greece. Has it worked since?" This is Bertie's voice — he has a temper that dampens his stutter, but also wit and an appreciation for the witlessness of the people who surround royalty. This will become important later.

Bertie dismisses the medic, then tells Elizabeth — with almost no stutter — that he is finished with speech therapy. Ignoring her husband's edict, Elizabeth has herself driven to a ratty Georgian house. The elevator is cantankerous, the waiting room empty and in some disrepair — and unconventional speech therapist Lionel Logue yells at her from the loo that he'll be right with her. This is a kind of informality with which Elizabeth is entirely unfamiliar. When Lionel appears, he has a slightly disreputable air, but his first line is from Shakespeare, "Poor and content is rich and rich enough." Elizabeth sees immediately that this mildly uncouth gentleman is no fool.

Lionel has no idea who Elizabeth is, but he is very confident he can cure her husband even though she explains that he has tried and failed with every other therapist. "I'm sure of anyone who wants to be cured," he says. Elizabeth replies, "He must be cured," and reveals her husband's identity. She demands that their sessions must be impersonal, private, and at Bertie's residence. Lionel refuses. "My game, my turf, my rules," he says. "I can cure your husband. But for my method to work there must be trust and total equality in the safety of my consulting room. No exceptions." Elizabeth agrees to it.

Note how audacious Lionel is, demanding "equality" with a royal. Trust and equality will be major **themes** in the film.

In my mind — although there are several candidates — I think that Elizabeth's first meeting with Lionel is the film's **inciting incident**, the event that spins the action into a whole new direction. Although it does not involve our protagonist, she takes the meeting on his behalf and it is only a matter of time before she drags Bertie to the same waiting room.

At York House we meet Bertie and Elizabeth's children Lilibet (10) and Margaret Rose (5). Bertie has almost no stammer reading to them, but it returns when he has to improvise — in this case a lovely story of a Prince turned into a penguin trying to get back to his daughters. Bertie's love for his family is evident in the scene — more of his everyday life spelled out. But also, we get the sense that the stutter is selective and only plagues him when the pressure is on.

Elizabeth tells Bertie she's found a new therapist she likes. He won't even discuss it.

Lionel auditions for a Shakespeare play but is refused the part because the director "... didn't hear the cries of a deformed creature yearning to be King." A fantastic line, I thought, given that Lionel is about to hear the cries of a dysfunctional royal yearning to be anything but King.

Elizabeth brings Bertie to meet Lionel. Notice that Seidler skipped the scene (or scenes) in which Elizabeth convinced her husband to go. The fact that Bertie shows up implies that she worked her magic; exactly how was not really relevant to the story. We understand that she is persistent and that she cares deeply for her husband's wellbeing, and that is enough. Interestingly, much later in the piece Elizabeth tells Bertie she only married him because his stutter meant she would never be trapped into royal service, so we understand by implication what a selfless partner she is to him.

Bertie's introduction to Lionel is the film's **first plot point**. Their first scene together is delicious and proves without a shadow of a doubt that Lionel is different from anyone Bertie has yet encountered. The scene spans six pages, really long for a scene comprised entirely of talking. (Three pages is a standard maximum.) But so much happens — there are so many reversals, so much set up:

- Lionel wants to know about Bertie's earliest recollections, but Bertie makes personal conversation off-limits. They are not to be friends.

- Lionel asks what he's doing there. "Because I bloody well stammer!" says Bertie, showing his temper.

- Lionel will not accept Bertie's assertion that he always had a stammer. He insists that something in his past caused it, and we understand that the film will carry us to a point where that secret will be revealed.

- Lionel makes Bertie a bet — a shilling and the right to question him if Lionel can prove he can get Bertie to "...read flawlessly, right here, right now." Bertie, of course, has no money on him, but Lionel is willing to stake him. Lionel records Bertie reading Shakespeare while wearing headphones blasting music that blocks out Bertie's own voice. (This is where we see that Bertie and Lionel share a dim view of royals: When Bertie objects to the headphones Lionel says, "Surely a Prince's brain knows what its mouth is doing," to which Bertie replies, "You're not well acquainted with Royal Princes, are you?" This particular dry wit becomes part of their budding friendship.)

• Bertie finishes his reading certain he failed. Lionel assures him he was sublime, but Bertie storms out of there, telling Elizabeth he's finished. Lionel gives him the recording to take home.

In the King's Study, Bertie watches his father King George V broadcast his Christmas address. Afterward, George insists that Bertie try the microphone. It is another brilliant scene that presents the **stakes**...

> KING GEORGE V
> This devilish device will change
> everything if you won't. In the past all
> a King had to do was look respectable in
> uniform and not fall off his horse. Now we
> must invade people's homes and ingratiate
> ourselves with them. This family is
> reduced to those lowest, basest of all
> creatures...we've become...actors!

> BERTIE
> Papa, we're not a family, we're a firm...

His father shoots Bertie a surprised look: does the lad have a brain after all?

> KING GEORGE V
> The most successful institution in
> history. Our cousins wear crowns
> throughout Europe. A dozen of them!
> Sitting on thrones is our business! Yet
> any moment some of us may be out of work.

Your darling brother... The only wife he
appears interested in is invariably the
wife of another!

> BERTIE
> (tries to brighten things)
> He's broken off with Lady Furness.

> KING GEORGE V
> And taken up a *Mrs.* Simpson, a woman with
> two husbands living! Had the audacity to
> present her to me at Georgie's wedding.
> I told him straight no divorced person
> could ever be received at court. He said
> she made him sublimely happy. I imagined
> that was because she was sleeping with
> him. "I give you my word we've never had
> immoral relations," he replied. Stared
> square into his father's eyes... *and
> lied*. When I'm dead that boy will ruin
> himself, this family, and this nation,
> within twelve months. Who'll pick up the
> pieces? Herr Hitler, intimidating half of
> Europe, Marshall Stalin the other half?
> Who'll stand between us, the jackboots,
> and the proletarian abyss? You? With your
> older brother shirking his duties, you're
> going to have to do a lot more of this.
> (nodding towards the microphone) Have a go
> yourself.

Bertie tries to read the King's speech.

> BERTIE
> Through one of the m—

KING GEORGE V

Get it out boy!

Even — or perhaps especially — understanding all that is at stake, Bertie is unable to speak. His father tries encouraging him but finally loses all patience and yells, "Do it!"

There is a lot to study in this scene. For one thing, the King, though he proves himself to be a boor as a father, is shown here to be prescient and wise — this is no fool, no black-and-white character.

Also, of course, Bertie understands that his father is very likely right about both the world and the fate of his brother. He leaves distraught — he is in real crisis.

At home, Bertie is still certain that Lionel lied to him, but puts on the recording as an act of self-torment — and is stunned to discover that Lionel was in fact telling the truth: Unable to hear himself, he read perfectly. This is the **end of Act One**, when Bertie decides to pursue the opportunity Lionel presents.

Do you know that children's game in which you put thumbs to the forefingers of opposite hands together and then "walk" your hands up by rotating around the top pair so the bottom is now above it? This is the image I have of how good screenplays work, this process of one reversal after another. Look at Act One of *The King's Speech* as an example:

- Bertie fails when his father demands that he broadcast a speech. Total humiliation. Speech therapy fails and Bertie decides he will do no more of it. He is hopeless — a low point. BUT THEN...

- Elizabeth discovers one more therapist, this one so eccentric and confident that there is renewed hope. This is upbeat. THEREFORE...

- Bertie visits Lionel but storms out in frustration. Reaffirms his conviction that he is a hopeless stutterer. Downbeat. BUT THEN...

- Bertie fails once more before his father, who explains to him that with his older brother proving to be a flake and with Hitler about to storm Europe, Bertie will have to step up to the plate. A crisis point. BUT THEN...

- Bertie discovers Lionel might really be able to cure him. Reluctant optimism.

Act Two opens with Bertie and Elizabeth back in Lionel's studio. They remain insistent that there should be "no personal nonsense." Lionel is not surprised that Bertie has not brought the shilling he owes. He agrees to work only on the mechanics of speech, but says they will need to meet every day. Bertie agrees.

What follows is a montage of Bertie and Elizabeth in Lionel's studio with Lionel putting Bertie through various physical exercises to build strength and encourage relaxation. Lionel is quite funny and irreverent, but it is not clear that he is getting through to Bertie.

Then Bertie and Elizabeth visit a factory. At first Bertie's speech is covered by the noise of the machinery and it works like the music in the headphones did. It takes a while after the machinery is silenced for the quiet to seep in and the stammer to reappear. But Bertie slows down and gets through his speech, an encouraging moment.

Bertie's older brother David flies in because their father is ill. David is all arrogance and bluster, and he is mad at his father for being so inconsiderate as to fall ill. He speaks of Wallis Simpson as "terribly clever."

Bertie finds his father frail and confused. Leaving his father's side, he finds David on the phone with Wallis, reluctant to hurry to dinner with their mother — Queen Mary. Mary is disgusted by David and says that if George was well none of his silliness would be tolerated. Archbishop Cosmo Lang tries to brown nose David but it goes largely unnoticed.

When King George V dies, David says, "I hope I will make good as he has made good," and then sobs in his mother's arms. Later, Bertie asks what the hell that was all about and David whines, "Poor Wallis. Now I'm trapped." Even upon his father's death he is only thinking of himself. Bertie must have a premonition that his father was right and that he is going to be called upon in some unexpected way.

This is, of course, a huge moment in the screenplay. Everything changes now and is focused on the succession. We are on page 39 of a 90-page script. Is this the midpoint? Well, it is certainly the turning point that leads to David abdicating the throne. It for sure puts Bertie in greater conflict with his brother as he watches him misbehave. But while it flips the film around, I am not sure it spins Bertie's story enough to be the true midpoint.

In his consultation room, Lionel listens to the radio report of George's death while his kids ask him to test them on their knowledge of Shakespeare, reminding us of Lionel's first love. Bertie shows up unannounced, tells Lionel he's been practicing despite all that has happened. Lionel offers him tea, but Bertie wants something stronger. Drinking together, Lionel confesses that he is haunted by being absent at his father's death. (His dad was a brewer.)

Bertie reciprocates with a confession of his own. "I was informed, after the fact, my father's last words were: 'Bertie has more guts than the rest of his brothers put together.' He couldn't say that to my face." Then he blurts, "My brother. That's why I'm here." When he is unable to continue, Lionel tells him to sing his words to his favorite song ("Swanee River") but Bertie refuses. When Bertie proves entranced by the model planes Lionel's kids are building, Lionel says he can work on one if he sings.

Lionel asks Bertie how it feels now that David is on the throne. Bertie replies, "It was a relief... Knowing I wouldn't be King."

> LIONEL
> But unless he produces an heir, you're
> next in line. And your daughter,
> Elizabeth, would then succeed you.

> BERTIE
> You're barking up the wrong tree now,
> Doctor, Doctor.

> LIONEL
> Lionel, Lionel. You didn't stammer.

> BERTIE
> Of course I didn't stammer, I was singing!
> (realizes)
> Oh...

So Lionel has made even more progress convincing Bertie that his eccentric methods work — and that Bertie is curable.

Bertie reminisces about how close he and David were as boys. But when Lionel asks if David teased him, Bertie admits, "They all did," and were even encouraged to do so by their father. Lionel, meanwhile, has been watching Bertie work on the model plane and asks if he's naturally right-handed. Bertie admits he was punished when he used his left hand, a common history with people who stammer. He also wore terribly painful braces to correct his knock knees. But the worst came at the hands of his nanny.

> LIONEL
> Who were you closest to in your family?

> BERTIE
> Nannies. Not my first nanny, though...
> she loved David...hated me. When I was
> presented to my parents for the daily
> viewing, she'd...

> The stammering produced by the memory halts
> him.

> LIONEL
> Sing it.

> BERTIE
> (tunelessly)
> "She pinched me so I'd cry and be sent

```
away at once, then she wouldn't feed me,
far far away."
     (speaks)
Took three years for my parents to notice…
```

After a bit more conversation about Bertie's younger brother who died at 13, hidden from view because the family was embarrassed by his epilepsy, Bertie says:

```
             BERTIE (CONT'D)
You know, Lionel, you're the first ordinary
Englishman...

             LIONEL
Australian.

             BERTIE
...I've ever really spoken to. Sometimes,
when I ride through the streets and see,
you know, the Common Man staring at me,
I'm struck by how little I know of his
life, and how little he knows of mine.

             LIONEL
What're friends for?

             BERTIE
I wouldn't know.
```

We are now on page 46 out of 90 pages — almost exactly half way. This is an astonishing scene. Both Lionel and the reader are made to feel such sympathy for Bertie's loneliness. The scene functions rather like a love song in a musical that somehow bridges the distance between strangers and lovers in the course of a single song. In this case, the bereaved future King of England has no one else to turn to except for his eccentric speech therapist, who has done little more than insist that Bertie be himself. The **major emotional relationship** in the film is between Bertie and Lionel. Bertie's decision to visit Lionel here is that story's midpoint.

Lionel, his wife Myrtle and their sons attend the funeral of King George V. Lionel remarks that the irony of the moment is that the sons did not like the father, then conceals from Myrtle how he knows that — He has kept his promise to Bertie and told no one, not even his wife, of his new client's identity. But amidst all the pomp and circumstance Lionel really sees for the first time the enormous importance of the work he is doing.

Bertie and Elizabeth join a dinner party with David and Wallis. They are appalled by the fact that David has had ancient trees chopped down to improve his view. David is oblivious to the travesty, but worse, he is oblivious to the machinations of Wallis as she ostentatiously forces him to fetch her more champagne instead of allowing a servant to do it. Churchill, though, is appalled and in a private conversation with Elizabeth basically calls Wallis a whore.

Bertie attempts to have a real conversation with David about his responsibilities as King but all David will talk about is his intention to marry Wallis once she is divorced. Bertie says it is impossible and David gets really nasty, accusing Bertie of trying to push him from the throne. Bertie tightens up and is unable to make a reply.

Back with Lionel, Bertie is enraged he couldn't get a response to David's insult out — and in his rage his stutter vanishes. Lionel gets Bertie to curse. No stutter there, either, but Lionel's young son overhears and so Lionel suggests they go for a walk. Bertie puts on a disguise.

In the park, Bertie replays his conversation with David, and Lionel concludes that that will leave Bertie King. "A damn good King, too," he insists. When he sees Bertie's upset by the thought, he touches him in a gesture of comfort, but Bertie goes bonkers, declaring the session over and calls Lionel "...the disappointing son a of a brewer."

Things go from bad to worse when Prime Minister Stanley Baldwin explains to Bertie that, with Wallis twice divorced and known to be sleeping around on the King, the government will have to resign unless David abdicates. It is a great dramatic moment that elicits a statement of the choice that faces Bertie. He asks, "Prime Minister, you'd leave the country without a government?" And the Prime Minister responds, "Does the King do what he wants, or does he do what his people expect him to do?" What a terrible trap for Bertie to face.

Seidler keeps this theme going: At home, Lionel is truly distraught. He still hasn't revealed the name of his client, but tells his wife, "This chap truly could be somebody great, and he's fighting me." Myrtle replies with great wisdom, "Perhaps he doesn't want to be great. Perhaps that's what you want." When Lionel admits he might have overstepped, Myrtle tells him to go apologize. But Bertie refuses to see him.

Bertie sees Churchill, who further discusses David's irresponsibility, which Churchill says is especially troubling with war coming. Bertie is surprised Churchill is so certain of war — the bad news keeps piling on. Churchill suggests that when he becomes King he should call himself George VI.

It is on page 62 that David abdicates. This is an interesting moment. It feels like it must be Bertie's low point — how can things get any worse? And yet Seidler has more in store for him. On the way to the Accession Council Chamber he sees Lionel in the crowd but can't meet his eyes. But then he tries to address the high commissioners who have just handed him his Accession speech — and he can't get the words out. "He bows his head in humiliation. And shame."

At home things are being packed up for the move to Buckingham Palace. Bertie appears straight from his humiliation and is desperate for a hug. But his daughters curtsy instead and call him, "Your Majesty."

Later that night, Elizabeth finds Bertie trying to understand a stack of state papers. Broken, he confesses, "I'm not a King. I'm a naval officer. It's the only thing I know about." He sobs. This is the **"all is lost" moment.**

It is Elizabeth who helps him find his bearings:

```
Elizabeth speaks softly, with growing strength,
having already accepted and adapted to the
situation.
```

> ELIZABETH
>
> Dear, dear man... I refused your first two
> marriage proposals, not because I didn't
> love you, but because I couldn't bear
> the royal cage. Couldn't bear the idea
> of a life of tours and public duties,
> a life that no longer was really to be
> my own. Then I thought...he stammers so
> beautifully...they'll leave us alone.

She takes his anguished face in her hands
tenderly.

> ELIZABETH (CONT'D)
> But if I must be Queen, I intend be
> a very good Queen. Queen to a very
> great King indeed.

This is such a moving moment — this most private and insecure man is so beloved by those closest to him. His wife — even his awful father — recognized his greatness. Only Bertie does not.

We are at the **second plot point**: The one final opportunity to save the situation lies with Lionel. Bertie and Elizabeth visit him at his home. Alone in the study, Bertie apologizes to Lionel and finally presents him with the shilling he owes. He is terrified of what the future holds, but Lionel swears he will not allow Bertie to backslide. Lionel tells him he needn't be afraid of his father and brother — but then Myrtle returns home and Lionel wants to hide because he never told her the truth. Myrtle is shocked to discover royalty in her house. Bemused, Bertie throws open the doors to the study. Myrtle takes her revenge by inviting the royal couple to dinner but Elizabeth politely refuses.

I want to pause here to (finally) discuss the film's **antagonist** — this was, after all, the reason I wanted to write this analysis in the first place. There are a number of candidates at this point. There is the

British monarchy, which wants to enslave Bertie in a life of pomp and circumstance. There is Lionel Logue, with whom Bertie constantly spars. There is Bertie's brother David, who out of selfishness condemns him to the fate he fears. There is the stutter itself. But through all the sparring Lionel is never other than Bertie's ally. Bertie is frightened of the monarchy for sure and the film is laced with both jokes at the expense of royals and with people expressing horror at the life of a monarch. But Bertie must face his duty as King, not defeat the monarchy. As to his stutter — well, it seems to me that the stutter has no intent and is in any case merely a symptom.

The real antagonist is named on page 66 of the screenplay:

<pre>
                    BERTIE
If I fail in my duty... David could come
back. I've seen the placards "Save Our
King!" They don't mean me. Every other
monarch in history succeeded someone who
was dead, or about to be. My predecessor
is not only alive, but very much so. What
a bloody mess! I can't even give them a
Christmas Speech.

                    LIONEL
Like your Dad used to do?

                    BERTIE
Precisely.

                    LIONEL
Your father. He's not here.

                    BERTIE
Yes he is. He's on that bloody shilling I
gave you.

                    LIONEL
Easy enough to give away. You don't have
to carry him around in your pocket. Or
</pre>

```
          your brother. You don't need to be afraid
          of things you were afraid of when you were
          five.

      A pause -

                    LIONEL (CONT'D)
          You're very much your own man, Bertie.
          Your face is next, mate.
```

To me, Bertie's father King George V is the antagonist of the film. David is also named by Lionel, and indeed David participated in teasing Bertie as a child and by his self-indulgence forced Bertie onto the throne. But it was the father who encouraged his kids to tease Bertie about a stutter that had already taken hold, who had no tolerance for Bertie's weakness. It was the father, Queen Mary tells us in her dinner scene with Bertie and David, who ruled the roost, who forced Bertie to be right-handed and wear his leg braces and, we infer, ignored the signs that Bertie's nanny was abusing him. It is the ghost of King George the V who Bertie must defeat in the finale.

And so, armed with his friend and therapist, Bertie enters **Act Three.** Preparations are underway at Westminster Abbey for the coronation. A very snooty Archbishop Cosmo Lang tries to shoo Lionel from the room, but Bertie insists that Lionel will be seated in the King's box. Lang says, "But members of your family will be seated there, Sir." And Bertie replies, "That is why it's suitable." A lovely statement of the friendship that has grown between the two men. But when they force the Archbishop to leave so Bertie can practice in privacy, Bertie confronts Lionel about the fact that he isn't really a doctor. Lionel confesses that it's true, but also says he is gifted enough to have given traumatized soldiers their voices back. Frantic, Bertie says he should lock Lionel up on charges of fraud for "saddling this country with a voiceless King." Lionel has the audacity to sit on the chair that every King and Queen has sat upon at their coronation. Bertie rails at him...

BERTIE (CONT'D)
It'll be like mad King George the Third,
there'll be Mad King George the Stammerer,
who let his people down so badly in their
hour of need!

Lionel sits down on the chair of Edward the
Confessor.

BERTIE (CONT'D)
What're you doing? Get up! You can't sit
there!

Overlapping LIONEL
Why not? It's a chair.

BERTIE
No, it's not, that is Saint Edward's
Chair-

LIONEL
People have carved their initials
into it!

BERTIE
That chair is the seat on which every
King and Queen-

LIONEL
It's held in place by a large rock!

BERTIE
That is the Stone of Scone, you are
trivializing everything-

LIONEL
I don't care. I don't care how many Royal
arses have sat in this chair-

                    Overlapping BERTIE
Listen to me... !

                         LIONEL
Listen to you?! By what right?

                         BERTIE
Divine right, if you must! I'm your
King!!!

                         LIONEL
Noooo you're not! Told me so yourself.
Said you didn't want it. So why should I
waste my time listening to you?

                         BERTIE
Because I have a right to be heard!

                         LIONEL
Heard as what?!

                         BERTIE
A man! I HAVE A VOICE!!!

                         LIONEL
     (quietly)
Yes you do. You have such perseverance,
Bertie, you're the bravest man I know.
And you'll make a bloody good king.

Bertie stares at him.

   As if to prove the point, Archbishop Cosmo Lang arrives at this
point ready to replace Lionel with someone of impeccable credentials.
When Bertie objects, Lang replies, "Your Majesty's function is to
consult and be advised. You didn't consult, but you've just been
advised." And Bertie tells him, "Now I advise you: in this personal
matter I will make my own decision."

Lionel puts Bertie through his rehearsal and Bertie is able to speak his three lines...

The actual coronation plays off camera — we only see it on a filmed newsreel. All went well but we know Bertie is still concerned: When his daughter sees Hitler on the newsreel and asks what he's saying Bertie responds, "I don't know, but he seems to be saying it rather well."

Prime Minister Baldwin resigns in disgrace for having been so wrong about Hitler's intent. Neville Chamberlain becomes Prime Minister. Baldwin leaves with the warning, "I'm afraid, Sir, your greatest test is yet to come." This re-sets the ticking clock and reminds us that the coronation with its few spoken lines was but a tiny test for Bertie.

The film comes full circle starting on page 79 when Chamberlain announces that England is at war with Germany. Bertie's private secretary hands him a nine-minute speech to the nation and Bertie says, "Get Logue here immediately." By the time Lionel arrives they only have forty minutes to work the speech. Bertie stutters badly.

                          LIONEL
        Turn the hesitations into pauses, and say
        to yourself, "God save the King".

                          BERTIE
        I say that continually, but apparently no
        one's listening.

                          LIONEL
        Long pauses are good: they add solemnity
        to great occasions.

                          BERTIE
        Then I'm the solemnest king who ever
        lived. Lionel, I can't do this!

                          LIONEL
        Bertie, you can do this!

                    BERTIE
    If I am to be King...where is my power?
    May I form a Government, levy a tax or
    declare a war? No! Yet I am the seat of
    all authority. Why? Because the Nation
    believes when I speak, I speak for them.
    Yet I cannot speak!

As though none of this had happened:

                    LIONEL
    Let's take it from the top.

And Bertie rehearses, inserting curses and bits of songs into the pauses.

I so love that Bertie, even under these circumstances, has the wit to claim that he says God save the King all the time but God is apparently not listening — that is such a wonderful, human touch. It is a terribly important lesson for screenwriters as well — serious moments do not always require humorlessness.

Bertie has not yet rehearsed the final paragraph when Elizabeth comes to tell him it's time. Bertie takes the same "death march" down the long tunnel toward the microphone as he did at the beginning of the film. Along the way, Churchill confesses that he had a speech impediment as a child. "I eventually made an asset of it," he says, and there is a moment of recognition between the two men.

They finally reach the booth. Elizabeth steps back with a wonderful smile as Bertie and Logue are sealed into the booth.

                    BERTIE
    No matter how this turns out, I don't know
    how to thank you for what you've done.

                    LIONEL
    Knighthood?

They smile.

```
                    WOOD (O.S.)
        Twenty seconds.

                    LIONEL
        Forget everything else and just say it to
        me. Say it to me, as a friend.
```

Bertie gives his speech. We see the entire kingdom listening, a great contrast to the "conversation" going on between the two men in the booth. The speech is not flawless, but it is good enough. Bertie's family could not be more proud. And we learn that Lionel was present for every subsequent speech the King made.

Lionel's line, "Say it to me as a friend," was a moment of real revelation for me. I felt in that moment not only the great friendship that had grown between these two men, but also the great love that had spring up between the screenwriter and his characters. I suppose this should be obvious, but this was a moment in which I discovered a whole new level to something I wrote about earlier in this book.

The literature on the craft of screenwriting talks a lot about the presence of a primary emotional relationship that impacts a film's protagonist. But there is this other, unspoken love story that is key to a script's success, and that is the love affair between a screenwriter and his or her characters and the world they inhabit. This struck me particularly hard as I read *The King's Speech*, but in thinking about it since I realized that it marks every great screenplay I have ever read. That love shows itself in the details, in the writer's patient exploration of his or her characters, in knowing their strengths, but also understanding and forgiving and often healing their weaknesses and wounds.

Look in *Little Miss Sunshine* at the way Sheryl (the mother) accepts her loser husband back into her bed after he returns from his failed attempt to rescue his dream of selling his book. Richard would have been so easy to hate — he has been so obnoxious in so many circumstances — and yet Michael Arndt presents him as noble and human and deserving of his terrified wife's compassion even through her disappointment.

Or look again at the language Arndt uses to describe ungainly Olive's utterly inappropriate dance in the finale: "Olive turns and strides up the stage, hands on hips, shoulders swinging with an absolute and spectacular physical confidence... She dances with a total command — an exuberant, even witty mastery of her body, the music, the moves, everything. Most of all, she's doing it for herself — for her own sense of fun — and the judges are instantly irrelevant."

The judges are instantly irrelevant because Olive, trained by her irreverent grandfather, doesn't care about them — she's up there because she loves to dance. This language is a love letter to Olive, but also to her crazy, heroin-addicted grandfather who trained her to act that way. Michael Arndt <u>loves</u> these people, and the consequences of that love are all over the script.

The King's Speech portrays the relationship between two deeply flawed characters. Bertie, who will become King George VI and help guide Britain through WWII, is a man who yearns for anonymous service to country but who is fated to become King. He is a man with a lot to say, but whose voice has been silenced by a cold and abusive family. Lionel Logue wants to be an actor — one of the more self-absorbed professions — but has discovered that his capacity to care deeply for others translates into an ability to return the voices to those too traumatized to speak for themselves. Bertie's stiffness is matched by his desperately hidden desire for human connection; Lionel's irreverence and refusal to accept anything in his relationship with the King but equal standing is probably what has kept him poor but is also the thing that allows him to puncture Bertie's brittle veneer.

Seidler gives these two flawed men wonderfully human women to love them, wonderful children to love, and matching codes of honor. He gives them each a deep sense of wounded pride. The humiliations Bertie suffered at the hands of his family are laid out in detail. We see less profound humiliations for Lionel at his unsuccessful audition as an actor, but when Bertie calls him a disappointment to his father it rings just true enough. Their final moments of triumph — establishing a successful friendship and a voice fit for a King — are huge because of how effectively Seidler has communicated his love for these two men. It is why a film about a stutter could attract such major talent and such a large and grateful audience.

Rules are made to be broken: The screenplay for *Lincoln*

So, as I was working on a concluding section for this book I wrote this summary:

- A great film is a compelling story interrupted by the plot.

- The plot is the journey that slams your protagonist up against his/her deepest fears or most profound flaw.

- Your protagonist is defined as the person who is uniquely unqualified for the journey on which you have set him/her.

And then I stood up and went to see *Lincoln*, written by Tony Kushner and based in part on a book by Doris Kearns Goodwin. I realized I wasn't quite finished with this book.

Lincoln is a terrific film of ideas in the mold of *Amadeus*. The acting, especially by Daniel Day Lewis and Sally Field, is astounding. But the film doesn't follow the modern conventions. Abraham Lincoln is not portrayed as the flawed or tortured man who rises to the occasion to reach his goal. He is not painted as the most unlikely man for the job. He is instead portrayed as the ONLY man for the job, a somewhat old-fashioned hero.

Lincoln's flaw, the thing that nearly defeats his dream of ending slavery and that probably ultimately gets him killed, is his gift — He is absolutely single-minded in his conviction that he not only must put a stake in the heart of slavery, but also that he has the power to do so. His wife Mary and some members of his cabinet believe that once he wins the Civil War he will have tremendous power to do what he wants; they are worried that he will squander that power by bringing to vote an important bill that is certain to go down to defeat in the House of Representatives. Others believe that if the bill passes, then the Confederacy will have no reason to end the terrible war that is claiming so many lives. They feel it is worth postponing a decision on the fate of slavery if such action will end the war. But Lincoln is convinced the time is now, and he demands support.

Lincoln never wavers from that position. Congressman Thaddeus Stevens, played with delicious relish by Tommy Lee Jones, calls Lincoln the most honest man in America, but Lincoln shows only one moment of hesitation in his relentless willingness to stretch the truth and walk at the edge of legality: Alone with his telegraph operator, Lincoln begins to send a message to General Ulysses Grant to allow the Confederate delegation to travel to Washington to present its peace plan even though he knows that if there is a real chance for peace before the vote then the 13th Amendment will die in the House. But his hesitation is brief, and he quickly decides to order Grant to stall the delegation in Virginia. That duplicity — his willingness to stretch the truth and even the law — very nearly loses the day, but Lincoln recovers with one last lawyerly move, promising a disgruntled House that there is no peace delegation in Washington when he knows full well that such a delegation exists, sincerely wants to end the war, and is only absent from Washington because he prevented their arrival.

What makes the character work isn't that he has flaws that make his triumph unlikely. He is fascinating in that he is sort of a dictator for good, pushing the boundaries of ethics to get his way until we have that one moment of concern that he has pushed too far. He is fascinating in the way Jack Nicholson's character from *A Few Good Men* was fascinating, making the point that we don't really want to know the truth about what needs to be done beneath the surface in order to protect our democracy. His triumph is unlikely not because he wavers or makes mistakes — his conviction and instincts are nearly superhuman — but because he is pretty much the only person who believes he can succeed. He faces tremendous opposition to the bill in the House. His cabinet is a reluctant participant in his battle, knowing that there is much less public support for ending slavery than for ending the war. The terrible sights that greet Lincoln as he tours battlefields might cause a lesser man to waver — but Lincoln remains convinced that slavery must end in order for democracy to flourish.

Ultimately, it is the force of Lincoln's conviction that carries the day. At least on the surface, Lincoln has no doubts whatsoever about the path he has chosen. We love Lincoln — or at least I loved Lincoln — not because I identified with him as a fellow flawed human, but because I so yearn for a leader of such powerful conviction and deft political skills in the service of right.

Structurally, Lincoln is a major rule-breaker. That makes sense — this was, after all, a film based on a script that was trimmed back from its original 550 pages. But in cutting it back the filmmakers basically assumed that we would know the events that would normally make up Act One. So the movie begins, after a brief prologue, at its first plot point, providing by implication what would usually be necessary Act One information...

- Prologue: A vicious, hate-filled battle between Black Union soldiers and White Confederate soldiers. The terrible cost of the war is underlined. Later, Lincoln is drawn into a conversation with four soldiers. He is reminded of his promise at Gettysburg "...that these dead shall not have died in vain." Both the battle and the conversation are placed as markers of the events that lead up to the inciting incident that occurred before the film began: Lincoln's election as President, the start of the Civil War, and his "want" — his determination to deliver the nation from slavery. Lincoln's words from Gettysburg, thrown in his face by a Black soldier, are an indication of how much remains to be done. THEREFORE...

- Lincoln has a nightmare. He describes it to his wife Mary "It's the speed that's strange to me," he says. "I'm used to a deliberate pace." It's a reminder of who he was before the film began. Mary recognizes that the dream is about the battle to pass the 13th Amendment before the war ends, begs him to drop it. Her point is that he will have near absolute power once he ends the war and so should avoid squandering his credibility on a bill that has no chance of passing the House. But Lincoln clearly disagrees...

- In a sweet scene with his half-asleep son, we learn that the Lincoln family lost a son — Willie — three years earlier.

- Lincoln attends the dedication of a new flag pole. In the carriage later, Secretary of State Seward makes the same plea Mary did. But Lincoln is again unmoved. In a scene in his office he refers to the election he just won that will give him a second term — note that the election also occurred before the film began. The election was in fact the first plot point in an Act One that took place in large measure before the film began. Lincoln now tells Seward that he sees opportunity in that election — sixty-four House democrats lost their seats, which means they are still around to vote, but after their term is up they will be looking for work. Lincoln wants to trade jobs for votes. Seward is against it. THEREFORE...

- ...when a couple called Jolly visit Lincoln to petition against some injustice, Seward uses the visit to demonstrate to Lincoln that Mr. and Mrs. Jolly only favor the 13th Amendment because it might end the war — but if there was a way to end the war without creating a whole class of free Blacks, then that would be much more desirable to them. Again, Lincoln is not swayed and pushes them to visit their Congressman to campaign for passage of the bill while he considers their petition.

- The tightrope Lincoln is on is clear — the bill has zero chance of passing if it looks like there is any other way to end the war. Seward finally acquiesces and says he'll find men shady enough to make the job offers in secret, but he and Lincoln agree that Lincoln will need to find a way to hold onto the Republican votes. This occurs on page 18 — we are now in Act Two.

- Act 2a begins with Lincoln negotiating with Republican power broker Preston Blair. Blair is not a member of the House, but he is a conservative Republican power broker who believes in abolishing slavery, not a radical like Congressman Thaddeus Stevens who thinks Blacks are and should be treated as equals. Blair offers to hold the Republican voting block together only if Lincoln will send him to meet with Confederate President Jefferson Davis to discuss terms of peace. Blair once again emphasizes that Republicans will only back the 13th Amendment if they are assured it represents the only path to peace.

- The race to pass the bill escalates when in a cabinet meeting Lincoln is told of the Army's plan to shell Wilmington with an overwhelming bombardment as a means to finally force surrender. This, of course, means that the clock is ticking on his wish to get the bill passed before the war ends. When the wisdom of pushing the 13th Amendment is again questioned, Lincoln confesses that the Emancipation Proclamation was a stretch from a Constitutional point of view and will probably be toothless after the war. He tells his cabinet in no uncertain terms that he expects their support in putting a permanent end to slavery. So Seward goes off to give a guy named Bilbo and his compatriots marching orders for trading jobs for votes.

- On page 34 the House debate begins. Now, everything is on the line for Lincoln.

- Lincoln's older son Robert comes home from college wanting to join the army. Meanwhile, the push to lock in Democratic votes is slow going.

- On page 46, Seward tells Lincoln he heard the rumor that Lincoln has secretly authorized Blair to confer with Jefferson Davis. Seward is appalled that Lincoln would do so without conferring with him, but Lincoln makes the case that he had to play along with Blair — he can't be seen as refusing to discuss peace.

- When Robert Lincoln begs his father for permission to enlist we see how great Lincoln is at avoiding unwanted conversations — he is political even with his family. Later, there is a very dramatic scene between Lincoln and Mary in which she wails that Willie's death was her fault, she let Lincoln's business keep her from noticing how sick her son was. We see that Lincoln has internalized his grief — but also we see the price those around him pay for this obsession.

- At a party Lincoln throws, Mary confronts Thaddeus Stevens, who she clearly views as a weasel. She reminds him of how loved her husband is, taunts him that it must be terrible to know that he will never be so beloved by the people. Later, Lincoln presses Stevens to moderate his radical views on full equality for Blacks on the floor of the House to give the bill a chance to pass. Lincoln is at his most eloquent and most persuasive.

- On page 60 the shelling of Wilmington commences. Casualties are mounting. The clock is ticking ever louder.

- Congressmen Wood and Pendleton are the most outspoken opponents of the 13th Amendment. Pendleton tells Wood to taunt Stevens when next he has the floor, get him to admit his true objective is equality and not just abolition. Pendleton promises to have every member of the press present.

- Pressure is brought to bear on some of the voters Bilbo has "bought" for Lincoln. Lincoln is far from having the number of votes he needs.

- In Virginia, General Grant demands revisions to the Confederate peace proposal before he'll pass it along to the President. The Confederate states want to negotiate as if they are a separate nation; Grant says the only thing that will fly is rebel surrender. But Grant communicates to Lincoln that the commission is sincere and that he's concerned about sending it home empty handed.

- Lincoln ponders a stack of pardons for deserters. His instinct is to grant them. Later, he nearly replies to Grant that he should send the commission on to Washington, but at the last minute changes his mind and orders Grant to hold the men up in Virginia. This is Lincoln's one big beat of hesitation in the film.

- Congressman Ashby, the sponsor of the bill to pass the 13th Amendment, begs Thaddeus Stevens to control his mouth when he speaks before Congress, to only claim that he is for equality under the law and not full equal rights for Blacks. On the House floor, Stevens is indeed taunted by Wood, but manages to hold the line at equal treatment under the law. Even Mary approves. Later, Congressman Asa Litton expresses disgust at what he sees as Stevens' sellout, but Stevens admits there is almost nothing he won't do to see that the amendment is passed.

- On page 81, Lincoln takes his son Robert to an Army hospital. Robert refuses to go in, understanding it is a ploy to get him to back away from his desire to enlist. Robert later follows a cart dripping blood and sees it emptied into a pit already filled with severed limbs. Robert is sick, but that doesn't stop him from telling his father that he will be unable to respect himself unless he enlists. Later, Mary is enraged with Lincoln. They have a terrible fight but he insists that they each must shoulder their own burdens. At the theater later, Mary tells Lincoln that she knows he is gambling that he can get the votes and end the war before anything can happen to Robert. She tells him that he can no longer depend upon Seward alone to procure the necessary votes; he must step in. "Because if you fail to secure the necessary votes, woe unto you, sir. You will answer to me." This is on page 87 and it feels like the stakes could not be any higher. We are considerably past the midpoint of the script, but this feels like the technical midpoint/start of Act 2b. Everything is on the line, it looks like the bill could be defeated, and Lincoln must up his game.

- For the first time, Lincoln joins Seward in a meeting with Bilbo and company. Seward is not pleased — he has wanted to keep Lincoln at arm's reach from the maneuvering to gain votes. But Lincoln has a scheme he wants put in motion...

- Stevens works his arm-twisting magic on some members of the House while Lincoln personally campaigns for votes. When his cabinet proves disgruntled at his methods he finally loses it, expounding on the notion that now is the moment to end slavery for all time in America and demanding that they get in line and deliver him the two remaining votes he needs.

- Page 99 sees the morning of the vote in the House. This is sort of the start of the "shootout at the OK Corral" moment and so should technically be part of Act Three. But screenwriter Kushner once again plays with his structure to increase the sense of drama. Note that we haven't had Lincoln's low point yet. What Kushner has done is lure us into believing we're at the finale — but then, before things can even get going, he has Congressman Pendleton fire what he hopes will be the kill shot when he takes the floor with "confirmation" that the delegation from the Confederacy is in Washington with a proposal for peace. All hell breaks loose, the Democrats demand a postponement until they can get a response from Lincoln, and it looks like the 13th Amendment's goose is cooked. This is Lincoln's low point — though it only lasts for the briefest moment. When Bilbo presents Lincoln with the note from Pendleton, Lincoln immediately responds...

LINCOLN
This is precisely what Mr. Wood wishes
me to respond to? Word for word? This is
precisely the assurance that he demands of
me?

Lincoln has seen one final opportunity and immediately scrawls his response. He doesn't hesitate — he almost never hesitates — and so we don't get from him that this is a desperate play worthy of being called the **second plot point**. But those cabinet members present in the room, knowing that there is indeed a peace delegation, point out that Lincoln could be impeached for what he has written.

• Back in the House, there is utter bedlam when Lincoln's response is read. Here's the scene:

INT. THE HOUSE CHAMBER AND BALCONY — AFTERNOON

Bilbo, pushing past the pages, runs in, holding the note, Ashley snatches it, reading as he makes his way to the podium. All eyes are on Ashley.

            JAMES ASHLEY
From the President:

The chamber falls silent.

            JAMES ASHLEY (CONT'D)
  "So far as I know, there are no peace
  commissioners in the city nor are there
  likely to be."

Applause, booing, furious discussion.

            GEORGE PENDLETON
  "So far as I know-"?! That means nothing!
  Are there commissioners from the South or
  aren't there?!

In the balcony, Mary looks to [her friend and maid] Mrs. Keckley.

            JAMES ASHLEY
  The President has answered you, sir! Your
  peace offer is a fiction!

>   GEORGE PENDLETON
> That is not a denial, it is a lawyer's
> dodge!
>
>   JAMES ASHLEY
> Mr. Haddam? Is your faction satisfied?
>
> Preston Blair, in the balcony, hesitates.
> He looks at his daughter, who gives him a
> questioning look: "Do you want this on your
> head?"
>
> Preston doesn't. He indicates to Haddam with a
> small shake of his venerable head: "Drop it."

And that's that. Pendleton and Wood know they've been outmaneuvered but there is nothing for them to do. They sit — and **Act Three** commences with the start of voting.

- So we are in the Act Three finale — but our protagonist is not even present. He is a passive player, able only to sit on the sidelines and hope that he has the votes. We are on page 105 of a 126-page screenplay when the voting starts — and the voting continues to page 113 with cuts to Lincoln and various others monitoring the proceedings as news is telegraphed from the House.

- The bill passes, of course, and there is much jubilation on the winning side. Thaddeus Stevens takes the bill home and presents it to his Black housekeeper, who turns out to be his lover. His line to her is a statement of the THEME of the film — "The greatest measure of the Nineteenth Century. Passed by corruption, aided and abetted by the purest man in America." Later, in bed, he has her read the bill to him.

- Lincoln finally meets with the peace delegation. They want only to know if the Southern states will be admitted back into the union in time to vote against ratification. But Lincoln assures them he has the necessary number of states lined up. "The freedom to oppress" is over.

• Lincoln tours a final battlefield, an endless swath of dead soldiers from both sides. Later, he meets with General Grant. Lincoln says, "We've made it possible for one another to do terrible things." To which Grant responds, "And we've won the war. Now you have to lead us out of it." Lincoln says that after surrender the Confederate officers and soldiers should just be sent home. No punishment.

• Robert E. Lee surrenders. Leaving Grant's camp, he doesn't know what to do or how to act. But Grant leads his men in removing their hats in a show of respect. Lee is moved, slightly tips his in return, and departs.

• In a carriage, Mary tells her husband...

                    MARY
    All anyone will remember of me is I was
    crazy and I ruined your happiness.

                    LINCOLN
    Anyone thinks that doesn't understand,
    Molly.

She nods; then, tenderly:

                    MARY
    When they look at you, at what it cost
    to live at the heart of this, they'll
    wonder at it. They'll wonder at you. They
    should. But they should also look at the
    wretched woman by your side, if they want
    to understand what this was truly like.
    For an ordinary person. For anyone other
    than you.

```
Lincoln laughs, takes her hand. She leans
against him.

                    LINCOLN
    We must try to be happier. We must. Both of
    us. We've been so miserable for so long.
```

So Kushner has summed up his point of view — the war has taken a terrible toll on everyone but even Mary acknowledges that Lincoln is a superman.

• Lincoln is with his cabinet. He seems on the verge of backing suffrage for Blacks. But then he leaves for the theater with Mary and is assassinated. The film ends with a flashback to a speech Lincoln gave, a plea for the nation to bind its wounds and move on.

Lincoln is a terrific film. Tony Kushner, who won the Pulitzer Prize for his play *Angels in America*, received rave reviews and an Oscar nomination for this screenplay. But I would argue that it is a flawed work. Not because of the ways that it plays with the rules. But because it doesn't, at the end of the day, execute on its own ideas.

The film, at least in my view, isn't really so much a character drama — how can it be one when its protagonist never has any real moments of doubt? — as it is a film of ideas. Just as *Amadeus* posed the question, "Is God fair?" *Lincoln* wants to pose the question, "When do the ends justify the means?" Lincoln's primary character contradiction is that he is "the most honest man in America," but also one willing to stretch that honesty nearly to the breaking point in order to accomplish what he believes is right. In my mind, that should have provided for a much richer audience experience than it did. Why didn't it work?

Amadeus worked to some degree because it gave us the contrast between court composer Salieri's pious petitioner of God and Mozart's buffoonish recipient of God's gifts. *Lincoln*, on the other hand, provides no such contrast. There is no one who opposes Lincoln who also has his gifts. As written, opponents Wood and Pendleton seem to be little more than racists determined to keep Blacks enslaved. The only opponent who makes a real case is one member of the Confederate peace delegation who remarks that emancipation will mean the end of the Southern economy.

Had there been an opponent who got real screen time and who was equal to Lincoln in the politics of the-ends-justifies-the-means, then the question of why we backed Lincoln's methods and abhorred the same methods when used by his opposition would have been an interesting one that really spoke to the theme of the piece. In other words, Lincoln the hero would have had an adversary worthy of the story being told. For me, this is where Kushner's screenplay and Spielberg's film disappoint. This only underlines one of the most basic questions you have to ask yourself: Is every scene in my screenplay an expression of its theme?

My critique aside, Tony Kushner is a remarkable writer. His dialogue is extraordinary. The screenplay is really worth studying for the way in which it moves through a tremendous amount of historical material. I think it took a writer of his skill and experience to bend the rules of structure as far as he did. But note — One way or another he managed to give us all of the key pivot points. Nothing of what I wrote in the previous chapter should be taken to contradict the necessity of learning what those pivot points are and how they are meant to function.

EXERCISE

Do what I just did

This was an exercise in Chapter One, but I want you to do it again now that you (hopefully) know a lot more about what to look for. Choose a film that you can both watch and read. Watch it, paying careful attention to why you think it either did or did not work as a film. What is it that makes you care (or not care) about the characters? About the story? About the visuals? Now go back and read the screenplay to see how much of that was actually on the page.

10 FINAL THOUGHTS:
Lessons from Bob Dylan and the Internet

He who works with his hands is a laborer.

He who works with his hands and his head is a craftsman.

He who works with his hands and his head and his heart is an artist.

— Saint Francis of Assisi

This quote is where I started this book. It is perhaps strange to think of Saint Francis of Assisi as a tour guide for the territory "behind enemy lines." But if you have made it this far through the book then you have, I hope, learned the important lesson that has been underscored for me in the process of writing it — that from a point of view of deep behind "enemy lines" the screenwriters we look for are those who value what they have to say and have the tools to get that onto the page. This book presents you with the steps to get from concept to polished draft. At the same time, I have tried to encourage you, as a plea from someone who has read an excess of screenplays empty of heart, to be artists. I make this plea knowing that paradigms are shifting and the rules of craft will need to keep pace. Even though we have been telling stories according to the same rules for thousands of years, how much will need to adjust to the demands of new media and shorter attention spans and media fatigue is anyone's guess. It is likely that the rules of structure will get embedded in other, less recognizable forms. But our hearts — our need for love, our desire for connection, our search for compassion, our fear of death, our search for meaning, our efforts to get laid — these are constant. So I am making a case here for learning the rules of story structure, but using them to speak TRUTH to your audience. I am making the case for the power of knowing what you are writing about. It is a tougher journey if you treat your own voice as sacred and go to the trouble to unearth and adhere to the gifts of your muses. But it is well worth the extra effort.

Some years ago, when I was at Ascendant Pictures, I had a meeting with a director of some note who announced that he wanted to make an action film "without all the boring parts." He meant without the character development, romance, etc. There is a temptation to look at this conversation as one of those ridiculous Hollywood moments that could become fodder for years of cynical cocktail party banter. But in some ways this director's idea was cutting edge and even prescient. Audiences were becoming savvy enough to often be way ahead of the filmmakers seeking to entertain them. Things needed to change for audiences who were becoming bored with convention and reluctant to spend money on entertainment when they could be entertained for free at home.

The morphing of trends is accelerating. I recently took a class in something called "gameification," the application of game design and technology to non-game environments. The point of the class was that education, workplace productivity, marketing, social networks — even traffic control problems — are all susceptible to gameification. I thought it was something worth knowing about for the future. But last weekend I read about a cable show that features a spinning dial from a safe in the titles. Audience members who are able to extract the combination can go to a web site, "spin" the dial, open the safe, and get additional material about or from the show.

You know what this means? The future is now.

If everything we do is trending toward "entertainment," if people are willing to accept a cinematic experience on an iPhone-sized screen, if people are able to cherry pick and watch only what interests them, is there some paradigm, some golden ticket, for screenwriters to use to make their work standout and relevant?

I believe that there is.

1998's innovative *Run Lola Run* was ahead of the pack. Writer/director Tom Tykwer took the position that he could sweep the audience along in his film by hitting all the right beats but doing so on the fly. He opened his film right on the statement of theme, delivered as text on the screen:

> We shall not cease from exploration
> And the end of all our exploring
> Will be to arrive where we started
> And know the place for the first time
> — T.S. Eliot, "Little Gidding" from *Four Quartets*

> After the game is before the game.
> — S. Herberger

After an energized credit sequence, Tykwer took us straight to the inciting incident, with everyday life only presented by implication. We see Lola's apartment during her frantic phone with her boyfriend Mani, a freshman courier for a drug dealer. Mani reveals that he has lost 100,000 Deutschemarks of the dealer's money and has twenty minutes to replace them or he's dead. This information — the inciting incident — is delivered only three and a half minutes past the credit sequence.

Lola promises to get the money, thereby announcing her want. The camera spins around her as the faces of possible sources for the funds appear around her. The first plot point comes when she focuses on the portrait of her father — that's her best chance. But Tykwer also underscores the stakes here when her dad shakes his head, "No." But Lola is off like a shot. This is approximately eight and a half minutes past the credits, and we are in to Act Two. The rest of the film rarely stops moving. The electronic score is rave-like. The visuals, the way the film is cut, all emphasize the kinetic.

The truth is, Tykwer did what my seemingly lunatic director had suggested — he made an action film with none of the boring parts. But he did so by making the "boring stuff" kinetic, not by eliminating it. And he did one other thing as well, and at the end of the day this was why the film had such strong resonance with its audience. He never lost sight of his theme — the entire film was an expression of that theme of how we spend our lives racing in circles.

I think my point is, there are lots of ways to deliver the key beats of story structure, lots of ways to freshen your approach so long as an audience has a way of getting what it needs to connect with your story, and so long as you stay *grounded*.

Back when I was touring with La MaMa Experimental Theater there was a cast member with a stunningly beautiful voice. Really, it was a remarkably pure instrument. But this singer/actress never found much of a career. Why? Because there was not a shred of emotion in that voice. She was delivering nothing but intonation and tone. Contrast that with the genre of singers who on some technical level can't sing worth a damn but who nevertheless deliver something utterly compelling. Take Bob Dylan, for example, whose voice I once heard described as sounding like "a hound dog trapped in barbed wire." Or listen to folksinger Dave Van Ronk's heart-achingly beautiful version of Joni Mitchell's "Both Sides Now," (*http://www.youtube.com/watch?v=KMhBdIu8gaI*) or Tom Waits singing "Heart of Saturday Night." (*http://www.youtube.com/watch?v=f7UHd7NVegE*) These are not great voices in the conventional sense of the term. But they move people. Why? Of course part of the answer is that they are putting melody to incredible poetry. But some of Dylan's early songs — "Subterranean Homesick Blues" springs to mind — are shapeless blobs that break all sorts of rules of craft. Yet Dylan was even then considered to be one of the great American singer/songwriters. Why?

This is not so easy to answer without sounding horrifyingly new-agey or old-hippyish. The short answer is that there is something "musical" in these voices that goes beyond the "pretty." These singers are craftsmen even if their craft produces something rough. But there is also Truth in those voices, a connection to something both primal and profound. Just as the Indonesians believe that the chimes and gongs of their gamelan orchestras make audible the eternal music that exists all around us, I would say that these voices are in some way plugged directly into some earth-force that delivers eternal messages beyond words from the gods — who, by the way, represent not just the spiritual but also the lustful, the warrior, the humorous, and the shadow.

As writers, you need to master the craft of storytelling and the rules of structure, but you also need to search for the ways in which you translate this connection — which you all have in you — onto the page. Maybe that is just a branch of craft that gives you the tools to access and translate the Truth behind your writing. The rules of structure might morph, forms may change, but the quest to speak Truth, to discover the universal — even in the most profane piece of silliness — is what will make facing the blank page in your lonely workspace worthwhile.

I want to point you toward a video posted on YouTube. This is the song "Stand by Me" posted by Playing for Change (*http://www. youtube.com/watch?v=Us-TVg4oExM*). As of this writing it has earned more than fifty million hits. I have watched it dozens of times and am emotionally overwhelmed each time. Why? I believe that, though it lacks a conventional story structure, this video tells a story that honors its message through an extreme version of what Tykwer did.

"Stand by Me" was written by Ben E. King, Jerry Leiber, and Mike Stoller and first recorded by King in 1961. This new production is part of a 2008 documentary called *Playing for Change: Peace Through Music*. It opens on Roger Ridley, a street musician on the Third Street Promenade in Santa Monica, California. Ridley introduces the song with a statement of theme: "This song says, no matter who you are, no matter where you go in this life, at some point you're going to need somebody to stand by you."

And then he plays his guitar lick and starts the song. We see that Ridley is playing by himself on the mall. The mouth through which this incredible, passionate voice emanates is missing a tooth. In the background of this first scene, shown just enough, is a shot of the recording engineer, and another of a father dancing with his young daughter in his arms.

The scene shifts to New Orleans, Louisiana, where Grandpa Elliot takes over the vocals. Elliot was born in 1944 and has been singing on the streets since he was six years old, and all of that history is in his bearded face. His voice is more gentle than Ridley's, but no less convincing as he sings, "I won't be afraid/No I won't shed a tear/as long as the people/come and stand by me…"

Through the magic of digital recording the first two voices intertwine in a duet for a few bars. Elliot finishes his chorus and we watch a jet soar into the air, and then we are in Amsterdam, Netherlands, where the phenomenal, singing-for-his-life Clarence Becker takes over from some back street. He is buoyed by the totally out-of-place Twin Eagle Drum Group from Zuni, New Mexico. Their drumming is the opposite of rock, a gentle pulse meant to connect the Native American players to their gods, but their gods seem to play well with the gods of these other musicians and the combination of voices and instruments is mesmerizing. It is interesting to note that Ridley is the only musician who doesn't wear headphones; everyone else needs to listen to his version so their overdubs will be in sync. This provides some remarkable visuals, like the Native American leader in primitive face paint and modern headphones.

The filmmakers keep adding remarkable musicians from all over the world. We get Francois Viguie playing tambourine from Toulouse, France; Cesar Pope on tenor guitar from Rio de Janero, Brazil; Dimitri Dolganev playing delicious cello riffs from Moscow, Russia; a beautiful bottleneck guitar solo by Roberto Luti from New Orleans. We discover that the drummer, Junior Kissangwa Mbuta, has been playing on a fire escape in the Congo and one of the bass players, Pokei Klaas, from a dirt street in what looks like a slum in Guguletu, South Africa, that does nothing to erase the look of utter peace from his face as he plays. We get glorious back-up vocals from a singing group called Sinamuya from Umlazi, South Africa; and the sax solo is from Stefano Tomaselli from Pisa, Italy. And finally, what is for me the most haunting moment of the piece — the tiny, tenor voice that sounds almost reluctant to leave the shelter of South African Vusi Mahlasela's vocal cords reprising, "I won't be afraid." And then we end back in Santa Monica with that father cradling his little girl as Roger Ridley winds down the song.

Okay. This is not exactly a new song. According to Wikipedia, there have been more than 400 recorded versions. So why has this version garnered north of fifty million hits on YouTube? Partly it's the great and newish application of digital technology used to gather all these great musicians onto one recording without asking any of them to leave their hometowns. But I would argue that the bulk of the appeal comes from the storytelling.

There are, I think, two simultaneous stories being told. One is the story of the making of the piece, though most of that is told by implication. In this story, we only play the third act. The video, as far as I can tell, started with an idea — music brings people together. The piece gently reminds us of the first two acts by occasionally showing that there are people behind the piece through quick shots of the filmmakers. But it also assumes that we know enough about how the world works to fill in the blanks — there was the idea, there was an opportunity to act on it, there were the months of prep and fundraising — we all know that, not reason to replay it for us. So the video works for the same reason that Tom Tykwer could open *Run Lola Run* without spending time on Lola's regular life — because the filmmakers trust that we have seen so much film and video that they don't actually need to present the first two acts.

For me, this story breaks down as follows:

- Regular life — This is the unseen world of the filmmakers going about their daily existence, trying to scratch out a living.

- Inciting incident — Someone noticed that though the world is shrinking we are feeling increasingly isolated. Their want, then, is to demonstrate the possibility of some sort of global community in which people are there for one another.

- First plot point — The realization that compact digital cameras and recording equipment makes collecting voices and images from around the globe feasible on a budget. And what better song to try it on than "Stand By Me"?

- Act Two starts with raising some money. Recording begins in Santa Monica, then the crew travels to New Orleans and to New Mexico. The midpoint is that jet taking off. The second half of Act Two is recording in Italy, Brazil, the Congo, South Africa, Russia...

- The obstacles — Everyone knows this project was not easy to finance. I'm sure logistics were a nightmare.

- Act Three — The filmmakers had all this footage and all these recordings. Now they had to battle the editing suite, find a shape for this thing that made their point. I'm sure there were some technical glitches. But the finished product — which is all that we see — is proof of triumph.

- Theme: The theme, made so convincingly by Grandpa Elliot at the beginning of the video and echoing with such pathos in the end by Vusi Mahlasela — and I'm willing to bet that the power of this took the filmmakers by surprise — turned out to be, "I won't be afraid." I'm betting they discovered this through the editing process.

The film's theme is totally embedded in the way it is cut together — the way each "scene" seems to build on what preceded it. It starts with Ridley singing his heart out. He is singing alone on the mall, he has an audience of one man and one child. His missing tooth tells us all we need to know of his everyday life. This guy is a great musician and his passionate rendition of the song, delivered to an audience of two, instills in the viewer both joy and a vague sense of unease. But then this world community of singers and musicians materializes around him, all moved by the same song, all adding their gifts to the mix. The music is great, the visuals are stunning — and the message is clear. Ridley is not alone. He has no cause to be afraid. And neither do we — we can see the power of that song in the closing shot of the father practically fused to the child he embraces. All of this is embedded inside the first story.

This is not storytelling that looks on the surface like it follows the rules outlined in this book. But I believe that the piece in fact delivers on all the necessary beats, some literally and some by implication — and that the piece works as well as it does because the filmmakers have remained true to their yearning to deliver the idea that was at the heart of the effort from the beginning, to give us a moment that proves that we are not alone, that we can be a global community, that we speak a common language through music — that we don't need to be afraid.

This video does not deliver a new idea — it is, after all, a variation on the theme of the Twenty-Third Psalm — "Even though I walk through the valley of the shadow of death, I will fear no evil, for You are with me..." But it is a new version in which the gods of music and technology reassure us, as God did in the Bible, that we do not walk alone through this life, and that peace and understanding are possible. The filmmakers were able to deliver an end product of such power because they never lost sight of the heart of their project. They knew they were touching on something primal and universal. They knew they were telling a love story of sorts. It was the power of that idea that carried the day.

My point is this: The rules of storytelling structure are vital to learn, but once absorbed, the way they are used is malleable and open to experimentation. You are allowed, even encouraged, to honor your audience's knowledge and experience in deciding how much you need to tell. The constant, the thing that is not malleable at all is this — examine your writing for the truth that is peeking through, hang onto it for all you're worth. It will allow you to experiment with your structure if that is your inclination and, more importantly, to put living flesh on that structure. It will make you a writer.

EXERCISES

Examine what you've learned

What follows is a slight variation on the exercises from Chapter One.

1. Write a few sentences describing the film you have written. Think of this as a sales pitch. Write about who the main characters are, highlighting what makes the protagonist particularly interesting. Write about his or her journey, highlighting the thing — the central contradiction — that makes that journey difficult.

2. Write a bit about what draws you to this subject and/or character.

3. Write about what you think is special about your treatment of this story.

4. Write a few sentences about what you think the film is about at its heart.

5. Explain who you think the audience is for the film you want to write. Talk about why.

6. Write out your ideal cast and director list.

ABOUT THE AUTHOR

**John Schimmel** has more than twenty years' experience as a Hollywood studio development and production executive and producer with Warner Bros., with Michael Douglas and Steve Reuther's company Douglas-Reuther at Paramount Studios, and as President of Production at Ascendant Pictures. He has worked on such films as *The Fugitive*, *Batman*, *Interview with the Vampire*, *Outbreak*, *Face/Off*, *Lucky Number Slevin*, and *Lord of War*. Prior to that he worked as a bass player in New York theaters, clubs, and studios, and was a co-creator and co-star of the Broadway musical *Pump Boys and Dinettes*, nominated for both Tony and Laurence Olivier awards. John currently teaches screenwriting at the University of California at Riverside's Low Residency MFA Program in Creative Writing and Writing for the Performing Arts and works as a story consultant for Cloud Imperium Games, a video game company launched by legendary game creator Chris Roberts (*Wing Commander*). John can be reached at *jschimmelwp@gmail.com*, or through his website, *www.ScreenplayConsultingServices.com*, which he runs with screenwriter/professor/author Jule Selbo.

SAVE THE CAT!®
THE LAST BOOK ON SCREENWRITING YOU'LL EVER NEED!

BLAKE SNYDER

BEST SELLER

He made millions of dollars selling screenplays to Hollywood and here screenwriter Blake Snyder tells all. "Save the Cat!®" is just one of Snyder's many ironclad rules for making your ideas more marketable and your script more satisfying – and saleable, including:

- The four elements of every winning logline.
- The seven immutable laws of screenplay physics.
- The 10 genres and why they're important to your movie.
- Why your Hero must serve your idea.
- Mastering the Beats.
- Mastering the Board to create the Perfect Beast.
- How to get back on track with ironclad and proven rules for script repair.

This ultimate insider's guide reveals the secrets that none dare admit, told by a show biz veteran who's proven that you can sell your script if you can save the cat.

"Imagine what would happen in a town where more writers approached screenwriting the way Blake suggests? My weekend read would dramatically improve, both in sellable/producible content and in discovering new writers who understand the craft of storytelling and can be hired on assignment for ideas we already have in house."
> – From the Foreword by Sheila Hanahan Taylor, Vice President, Development at Zide/Perry Entertainment, whose films include *American Pie, Cats and Dogs, Final Destination*

"One of the most comprehensive and insightful how-to's out there. Save the Cat!® is a must-read for both the novice and the professional screenwriter."
> – Todd Black, Producer, *The Pursuit of Happyness, The Weather Man, S.W.A.T, Alex and Emma, Antwone Fisher*

"Want to know how to be a successful writer in Hollywood? The answers are here. Blake Snyder has written an insider's book that's informative – and funny, too."
> – David Hoberman, Producer, *The Shaggy Dog* (2005), *Raising Helen, Walking Tall, Bringing Down the House, Monk* (TV)

BLAKE SNYDER, besides selling million-dollar scripts to both Disney and Spielberg, was one of Hollywood's most successful spec screenwriters. Blake's vision continues on *www.blakesnyder.com*.

$19.95 · 216 PAGES · ORDER NUMBER 34RLS · ISBN: 9781932907001

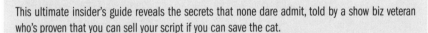

THE WRITER'S JOURNEY – 3RD EDITION
MYTHIC STRUCTURE FOR WRITERS

CHRISTOPHER VOGLER

BEST SELLER

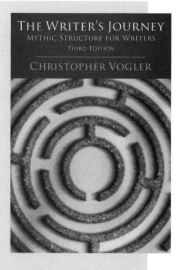

See why this book has become an international best seller and a true classic. *The Writer's Journey* explores the powerful relationship between mythology and storytelling in a clear, concise style that's made it required reading for movie executives, screenwriters, playwrights, scholars, and fans of pop culture all over the world.

Both fiction and nonfiction writers will discover a set of useful myth-inspired storytelling paradigms (i.e., "The Hero's Journey") and step-by-step guidelines to plot and character development. Based on the work of Joseph Campbell, *The Writer's Journey* is a must for all writers interested in further developing their craft.

The updated and revised third edition provides new insights and observations from Vogler's ongoing work on mythology's influence on stories, movies, and man himself.

"This book is like having the smartest person in the story meeting come home with you and whisper what to do in your ear as you write a screenplay. Insight for insight, step for step, Chris Vogler takes us through the process of connecting theme to story and making a script come alive."
> – Lynda Obst, producer, *Sleepless in Seattle*, *How to Lose a Guy in 10 Days*;
> author, *Hello, He Lied*

"This is a book about the stories we write, and perhaps more importantly, the stories we live. It is the most influential work I have yet encountered on the art, nature, and the very purpose of storytelling."
> – Bruce Joel Rubin, screenwriter, *Stuart Little 2*, *Deep Impact*,
> *Ghost*, *Jacob's Ladder*

CHRISTOPHER VOGLER is a veteran story consultant for major Hollywood film companies and a respected teacher of filmmakers and writers around the globe. He has influenced the stories of movies from *The Lion King* to *Fight Club* to *The Thin Red Line* and most recently wrote the first installment of *Ravenskull*, a Japanese-style manga or graphic novel. He is the executive producer of the feature film *P.S. Your Cat is Dead* and writer of the animated feature *Jester Till*.

$26.95 · 448 PAGES · ORDER NUMBER 76RLS · ISBN: 9781932907360

CINEMATIC STORYTELLING
THE 100 MOST POWERFUL FILM CONVENTIONS EVERY FILMMAKER MUST KNOW

JENNIFER VAN SIJLL

THE 100 MOST POWERFUL FILM CONVENTIONS EVERY FILMMAKER MUST KNOW JENNIFER VAN SIJLL

BEST SELLER

How do directors use screen direction to suggest conflict? How do screenwriters exploit film space to show change? How does editing style determine emotional response?

Many first-time writers and directors do not ask these questions. They forego the huge creative resource of the film medium, defaulting to dialog to tell their screen story. Yet most movies are carried by sound and picture. The industry's most successful writers and directors have mastered the cinematic conventions specific to the medium. They have harnessed non-dialog techniques to create some of the most cinematic moments in movie history.

This book is intended to help writers and directors more fully exploit the medium's inherent storytelling devices. It contains 100 non-dialog techniques that have been used by the industry's top writers and directors. From *Metropolis* and *Citizen Kane* to *Dead Man* and *Kill Bill*, the book illustrates — through 500 frame grabs and 75 script excerpts — how the inherent storytelling devices specific to film were exploited.

You will learn:
· How non-dialog film techniques can advance story.
· How master screenwriters exploit cinematic conventions to create powerful scenarios.

"Cinematic Storytelling *scores a direct hit in terms of concise information and perfectly chosen visuals, and it also searches out... and finds... an emotional core that many books of this nature either miss or are afraid of.*"
> — Kirsten Sheridan, Director, *Disco Pigs*; Co-writer, *In America*

"*Here is a uniquely fresh, accessible, and truly original contribution to the field. Jennifer van Sijll takes her readers in a wholly new direction, integrating aspects of screenwriting with all the film crafts in a way I've never before seen. It is essential reading not only for screenwriters but also for filmmakers of every stripe.*"
> — Prof. Richard Walter, UCLA Screenwriting Chairman

JENNIFER VAN SIJLL has taught film production, film history, and screenwriting. She is currently on the faculty at San Francisco State's Department of Cinema.

$24.95 · 230 PAGES · ORDER NUMBER 35RLS · ISBN: 9781932907056

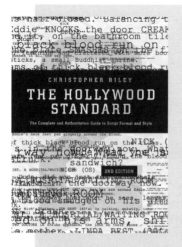

THE HOLLYWOOD STANDARD
2ND EDITION
THE COMPLETE AND AUTHORITATIVE GUIDE TO SCRIPT FORMAT AND STYLE

CHRISTOPHER RILEY

This is the book screenwriter Antwone Fisher (*Antwone Fisher*, *Tales from the Script*) insists his writing students at UCLA read. This book convinced John August (*Big Fish*, *Charlie and the Chocolate Factory*) to stop dispensing formatting advice on his popular writing website. His new advice: Consult *The Hollywood Standard*. The book working and aspiring writers keep beside their keyboards and rely on every day. Written by a professional screenwriter whose day job was running the vaunted script shop at Warner Bros., this book is used at USC's School of Cinema, UCLA, and the acclaimed Act One Writing Program in Hollywood, and in screenwriting programs around the world. It is the definitive guide to script format.

The Hollywood Standard describes in clear, vivid prose and hundreds of examples how to format every element of a screenplay or television script. A reference for everyone who writes for the screen, from the novice to the veteran, this is the dictionary of script format, with instructions for formatting everything from the simplest master scene heading to the most complex and challenging musical underwater dream sequence. This new edition includes a quick start guide, plus new chapters on avoiding a dozen deadly formatting mistakes, clarifying the difference between a spec script and production script, and mastering the vital art of proofreading. For the first time, readers will find instructions for formatting instant messages, text messages, email exchanges and caller ID.

"Aspiring writers sometimes wonder why people don't want to read their scripts. Sometimes it's not their story. Sometimes the format distracts. To write a screenplay, you need to learn the science. And this is the best, simplest, easiest to read book to teach you that science. It's the one I recommend to my students at UCLA."

— Antwone Fisher, from the foreword

CHRISTOPHER RILEY is a professional screenwriter working in Hollywood with his wife and writing partner, Kathleen Riley. Together they wrote the 1999 theatrical feature *After the Truth*, a multiple-award-winning German language courtroom thriller. Since then, the husband-wife team has written scripts ranging from legal and political thrillers to action-romances for Touchstone Pictures, Paramount Pictures, Mandalay Television Pictures and Sean Connery's Fountainbridge Films.

In addition to writing, the Rileys train aspiring screenwriters for work in Hollywood and have taught in Los Angeles, Chicago, Washington D.C., New York, and Paris. From 2005 to 2008, the author directed the acclaimed Act One Writing Program in Hollywood.

$24.95 · 208 PAGES · ORDER NUMBER 130RLS · ISBN: 9781932907636

{ THE MYTH OF MWP }

In a dark time, a light bringer came along, leading the curious and the frustrated to clarity and empowerment. It took the well-guarded secrets out of the hands of the few and made them available to all. It spread a spirit of openness and creative freedom, and built a storehouse of knowledge dedicated to the betterment of the arts.

The essence of the Michael Wiese Productions (MWP) is empowering people who have the burning desire to express themselves creatively. We help them realize their dreams by putting the tools in their hands. We demystify the sometimes secretive worlds of screenwriting, directing, acting, producing, film financing, and other media crafts.

By doing so, we hope to bring forth a realization of 'conscious media' which we define as being positively charged, emphasizing hope and affirming positive values like trust, cooperation, self-empowerment, freedom, and love. Grounded in the deep roots of myth, it aims to be healing both for those who make the art and those who encounter it. It hopes to be transformative for people, opening doors to new possibilities and pulling back veils to reveal hidden worlds.

MWP has built a storehouse of knowledge unequaled in the world, for no other publisher has so many titles on the media arts. Please visit www.mwp.com where you will find many free resources and a 25% discount on our books. Sign up and become part of the wider creative community!

Onward and upward,

Michael Wiese
Publisher/Filmmaker